Refined by Fire

Refined by Fire

How Trials Transform our Destiny

Deidra J. Young

Refined by Fire: How Trials Transform our Destiny

by Deidra J. Young

Copyright © 2025 by Deidra J. Young

Published by Wise Planning and Research Pty Ltd

Australia

All rights reserved

Unless otherwise indicated, all Scripture quotations are taken from the New King James Version of the Holy Bible.

Copyright © 1979, 1980, 1982 by Thomas Nelson, Inc., publishers. Used by permission.

Scripture quotations marked KJV are from the King James Version of the Bible.

This book or parts thereof may not be reproduced in any form, stored in a retrieval system or transmitted in any form by any means - electronic, mechanical, photocopy, recording or otherwise - without written permission of the publisher.

Illustrations are the property of by Deidra J. Young unless otherwise stated. All rights are reserved.

Cover design by: Deidra J. Young

Printed in Australia

ISBN: 978-1-7638014-1-7

And to the angel of the church of the Laodiceans write,

These things says the Amen, the Faithful and True Witness, the Beginning of the creation of God:

I know your works, that you are neither cold nor hot. I could wish you were cold or hot. So then, because you are lukewarm, and neither cold nor hot, I will vomit you out of My mouth.

Because you say, I am rich, have become wealthy, and have need of nothing and do not know that you are wretched, miserable, poor, blind, and naked. I counsel you to buy from Me gold refined in the fire, that you may be rich; and white garments, that you may be clothed, that the shame of your nakedness may not be revealed; and anoint your eyes with eye salve, that you may see.

As many as I love, I rebuke and chasten.

Therefore, be zealous and repent. Behold, I stand at the door and knock. If anyone hears My voice and opens the door, I will come in to him and dine with him, and he with Me.

To him who overcomes, I will grant to sit with Me on My throne, as I also overcame and sat down with My Father on His throne.

He who has an ear, let him hear what the Spirit says to the churches.

Revelation 3:14-22

Table of Contents

Chapter 1 Introduction 1

Chapter 2: The Refiner's Fire 9

Chapter 3: Trusting the Process 41

Chapter 4: The Purifying Flame 53

Chapter 5: Emerging Refined 70

Chapter 6: The Oil and Fine Linen 86

Chapter 7: The Laodicean Church Age 90

Chapter 8: The Baptism of Fire 96

Chapter 9: Is God Speaking to You? 121

Chapter 1 Introduction

O ur life is a journey towards Eternity, from conception in the womb to our death bed. Where are you planning to spend your Eternity?

What is your ultimate destination?

God knew our life, our families, our encounters (good and bad), our travels, who we would meet, who we would marry, our children, our pets, our parents and the difficulties we would experience. He has your life recorded in the *Book of Life (Revelation 3:5)*. Every encounter has been recorded. Every struggle is known to our Heavenly Father. There is nothing He does not know about you.

He is aware and feels every pain you suffer.

When our hearts are wounded by the words and actions of others, even our brothers and sisters in Christ, He sees this and sends comfort to our hearts. Every piercing, every jab, every wound is known.

While we are mostly unaware of the spiritual realm, we are so easily distracted by the cares and worries of this life. When we shift our gaze to Jesus, we can more easily see the spiritual realm. He is the author and finisher of our faith. Our faith is not built by anyone else but Him. The distractions and cares of this life can so easily lead us away from the one we love. It is the Lord who has provided the journey and He alone knows where we are headed.

Remember the two amazing women of God who welcomed Jesus into their home. They were devoted to Jesus. They were both Godly women and tried to serve Jesus in different ways.

Jesus exhorts us to be like Mary and listen to His words. He said that Mary had chosen the good part. What was that good part?

> *Now it happened as they went that He entered a certain village; and a certain woman named Martha welcomed Him into her house. And she had a sister called Mary, who also sat at Jesus' feet and heard His word.*
>
> *But Martha was distracted with much serving, and she approached Him and said, "Lord, do You not care that my sister has left me to serve alone? Therefore, tell her to help me."*
>
> *And Jesus answered and said to her, "Martha, Martha, you are worried and troubled about many things. But one thing is needed, and Mary has chosen that good part, which will not be taken away from her."*
>
> Luke 10:38-42

Mary chose to focus her thoughts and mind on Jesus, listening to Him. This is the true battle ground. As we travel through our lives, it is essential to maintain a focus on Jesus who keeps us on the path and provides heavenly rewards. Heaven's rewards are not mere earthly treasures, but eternal blessings that testify to God's unwavering love and justice.

Do not neglect to give the Lord the first fruits of your morning to Him (Psalm 55:17). Prioritise Him over your family, your household duties, your friends, your job and your work. Morning worship develops an intimacy that no other action on your part can develop.

Many think that true success on earth includes academic qualifications, prizes, awards, money, houses, land and fame. Maybe you own property or maybe you are sociable. This is simply a temporary life, for there is something far greater to strive for: to serve Him in our calling and to become like Him. When you pursue the Lord, He leads you and guides you throughout your life (Psalm 25:9).

Each of us has a unique purpose here on earth. You will find your purpose changes over the course of your life, but He makes the way clear to you. All you have to do is surrender yourself to Him, seek Him, call on Him and He will show you your purpose and your calling (2 Timothy 1:8-11).

In my own life, I have found my purpose changed dramatically with time. However, my calling and purpose in my younger life is not the same as my calling in my latter years.

Have you found your calling? Are you pursuing it?

I journeyed from a young woman devoted to Jesus at a very young age (16 years) being born again in a Sydney hospital. It was a life of character building and worship. Although through many failings, He rescued me out of them all.

One thing is clear in my life of service, there is a profound purpose in our pain and suffering. Just as gold is purified by intense heat and flames, our faith is refined through the fires of adversity (Isaiah 30:20-21). Not only our faith, but our character becomes purified as we travel.

There is a profound truth, which is not taught in many churches today. The message of character development.

Do not be deceived, for your character is not purified in revival, through anointing, in great fellowship and the moving of the Holy Spirit in church meetings.

Revival and anointings have a purpose in life, to encourage you and unite the body of Christ, but you will be most changed in your trials and sufferings.

True character is built and established by this one method (James 1:12).

Just as Jesus suffered for you and for me, so you are no greater than Him. It is part of our journey that we suffer just as He suffered.

The Apostle Paul wrote many of his letters from prison warned Timothy:

> *All who desire to live godly in Christ Jesus, will suffer persecution.*   *2 Timothy 3:12*

Living a godly life in Christ Jesus is not easy. Not just because we are living in this world, but because we are fighting a spiritual warfare.

> *For whatever is born of God overcomes the world. And this is the victory that has overcome the world - our faith. Who is he who overcomes the world, but he who believes that Jesus is the Son of God?*   *1 John 5:4, 5*

Peter says we should commit our souls to Him when we suffer. That He is faithful and true.

> **The Apostle Peter Warned the Church:**
>
> *Therefore, let those who suffer according to the will of God, commit their souls to Him in doing good, as to a faithful Creator.*   *1 Peter 4:19*

Finally, Jesus warned His Disciples (and us) that we are destined to be hated in this world. We are destined to be persecuted in this world. We are also destined to overcome this world.

Paul's letter to the Romans emphasized that we are not to be overcome by evil, but to overcome evil with good (Romans 12:21).

Jesus Warned His Disciples:

> *Remember the word that I said to you; a servant is not greater than his master. If they persecuted Me, they will also persecute you. If they kept My word, they will keep yours also. John 15:18-21*

The Apostle Peter wrote to the Jewish believers, who were struggling in the midst of persecution, to conduct themselves courageously:

> *In this you greatly rejoice, though now for a little while you may have had to suffer grief in all kinds of trials. These have come so that your faith - of greater worth than gold, which perishes even though refined by fire - may be proved genuine and may result in praise, glory and honour when Jesus Christ is revealed.*
>   *1 Peter 1:6-7*

Persecution can cause either growth or bitterness in the Christian life. Your response determines the result. In writing to Jewish believers struggling in the midst of persecution, Peter encourages them to conduct themselves courageously for the Person and program of Christ (1 Peter 4:12-13; 2 Timothy 3:12). Both their character and conduct must be above reproach. Having been born again to a living hope, they are to imitate the Holy One who has called them.

The Christians were not to think it strange concerning the fiery trial, as though some strange thing happened unto you, but rejoice as partakers of the suffering of Christ. That response to life is truly the climax of one's submission to the good hand of God.

> *Beloved, do not think it strange concerning the fiery trial, which is to try you, as though some strange thing happened to you; but rejoice to the extent that you partake of Christ's sufferings, that when His glory is revealed, you may also be glad with exceeding joy.*   *1 Peter 4:12-13*

You and I are no different. Peter encourages his beloved audience that it is not a strange occurrence. He even commands us to rejoice. In the same way, Jesus Christ wants to reveal Himself to us in our trials and sufferings.

Just as gold is purified and shaped by intense heat and flames, so we are refined through the difficulties and trials we face as believers (Zechariah 13:9). While suffering is never enjoyable, it serves the crucial purpose of burning away the impurities in our lives and tempering our faith into something radiant, genuine and precious (Romans 8:18).

Gold is forged in the blazing heat of the refiner's fire, our faith is tested and shaped by the flames of adversity we encounter (Malachi

3:2). From the devastation of broken relationships, death of a loved one, termination of your employment to the anguish of life-altering illness, from the pain of dashed dreams to the gut-wrenching trauma of loss – tribulations of every kind have the ability to either purify our faith to radiant beauty or leave it charred and diminished.

In the chapters ahead, we will explore the holy refining process in greater depth through the lens of Scripture. We will examine why trials are inevitable, yet necessary for spiritual growth as God's children. We will wrestle with what it means to surrender our lives to the refiner's fire rather than railing against adversity.

Further, we will unpack how suffering ultimately burns away the impurities in our lives – the pride, idolatry and selfishness that so often tarnishes our faith.

Ultimately, we will see that no tears, no tragedies, and no trials are wasted for those who entrust themselves to God. As we embrace God's holy process of being molten and shaped by fire, our faith emerges radiant, purified, and reflecting the very glory of Christ for all to see. Like gold refined by blazing heat to remove its impurities, our tested and transformed faith is revealed as something of far greater worth – the object of eternal "praise, glory and honour when Jesus Christ is revealed."

So let us journey together with hearts open and minds receptive to the purifying power of trials. For it is the embracing of the refiner's fire that produces a jewel of immeasurable value – a luminous, unshakable faith in the God who is making all things new.

Chapter 2: The Refiner's Fire

From the very beginning, God has made His intentions clear. He desires to purify and refine His people, not just outwardly, but at the very core of our being. Just as a refiner purifies precious metals through the scorching heat of the flame, so our heavenly Father subjects our faith to the refiner's fire of trials and adversity. It is through these blazing trials that the impurities and imperfections are burned away, leaving only what is precious, lasting, and beautiful.

> *But who can endure the day of His coming?*
> *And who can stand when He appears?*
> *For He is like a refiner's fire and like launderers' soap.*
>
> *He will sit as a refiner and a purifier of silver.*
> *He will purify the sons of Levi and purge them as gold and silver, that they may offer to the LORD an offering in righteousness.*
>
> *Malachi 3:2-3*

In the ancient process of refining gold and silver, the refiner would build a raging fire of intense heat. He would then place the rough ore containing the precious metal into a crucible - a ceramic vessel able to withstand the raging inferno. As the metal became liquid in the blasting furnace, the dross and impurities would be burned away and rise to the surface as scum to be skimmed off.

This fiery process was repeated until the refiner could see his own clear reflection on the glassy surface of the molten metal.

So, it is with us, as we endure the scorching trials and tribulations of this life. God, our divine refiner, places us into His crucible of refinement – the difficulties, pains, and adversities we encounter. While it is never enjoyable, the fires of affliction serve to consume the impurities within us, burning away the dross of sinful habits, selfish desires, and shallow faith.

The Refining Fire's Purifying Power

Throughout Scripture, we see example after example of God refining the faith of His people through blazing fire and extreme adversity. We see the raging flames of persecution separating the genuine faith of believers from the charred faith of pretenders and false converts. We see the intense heat of relentless trials transforming followers of Christ from spiritual immaturity into luminous witnesses of stunning Christ-like character. And we see the purifying fire of anguish stripping away idols, pride, and self-reliance, leaving only an unshakable foundation of complete trust and dependence on God.

For the faithful, the refiner's fire is always purposeful and intentional, tempering and tooling their faith into something radiant, authentic, and powerful. Through blazing trials and white-hot adversity, the divine refiner smelts away our spiritual impurities, burning off the worthless dross to reveal lustrous faith and character, tested and transformed to reflect the very glory of Jesus Christ.

Refining Examples from Scripture

The bible is filled with ordinary people of simple faith who were thrust into extraordinary crucibles of refinement. Just like you, their faith endured scorching trials and fiery adversity, revealing its radiance and worth through the very difficulties intended to destroy it.

One example is Job.

The enemy sought to attack Job and his faith in God's sovereignty remaining radiant and unshakable amid the tragic loss of his children, his wealth, and his health – all because God allowed the refining fires of incomprehensible pain to test the authenticity of Job's devotion.

You are no different to Job. His was a life full of blessings, prosperity and family. So blessed was Job, that the Lord bragged about him to Satan.

> *Then the LORD said to Satan,*
>
> *"Have you considered My servant Job, that there is none like him on the earth, a blameless and upright man, one who fears God and shuns evil?"*
>
> *Satan answered the LORD and said, "Does Job fear God for nothing? Have You not made a hedge around him, around his household, and around all that he has on every side? You have blessed the work of his hands, and his possessions have increased in the land. But now, stretch out Your hand and touch all that he has, and he will surely curse You to Your face!"*
>
> *And the LORD said to Satan, "Behold, all that he has is in your power; only do not lay a hand on his person." So, Satan went out from the presence of the LORD.*   *Job 1:8-12*

Satan took Job's possessions, his health and robbed him of his wife and family. Job was attacked with great brutality.

Yet through all of this, Job did not sin. Eliphaz said to Job that God was correcting him. Yet Job asserted that his friends were of no comfort. Even Bildad and Zophar told Job he should repent. Job was offended by his friends who did not embrace him. He responded that he had wisdom and understanding too. He had already been weeping before God over the calamities which happened to him.

> *I have sewn sackcloth over my skin and laid my head in the dust. My face is flushed from weeping, and on my eyelids is the shadow of death; Although no violence is in my hands, and my prayer is pure.*   *Job 5:17-18*

All of the utterances of Job and his friends were challenged by God who appeared in a whirlwind. While Job immediately repented, his friends had to repent as well. After all the sufferings of Job, God restored what he lost and granted him a long life.

> *So Eliphaz the Temanite and Bildad the Shuhite and Zophar the Naamathite went and did as the Lord commanded them; for the Lord had accepted Job. And the Lord restored Job's losses when he prayed for his friends. Indeed, the Lord gave Job twice as much as he had before. Then all his brothers, all his sisters, and all those who had been his acquaintances before, came to him and ate food with him in his house; and they consoled him and comforted him for all the adversity that the Lord had brought upon him. Each one gave him a piece of silver and each a ring of gold.*

> *Now the Lord blessed the latter days of Job more than his beginning; for he had fourteen thousand sheep, six thousand camels, one thousand yoke of oxen, and one thousand female donkeys. He also had seven sons and three daughters. And he called the name of the first Jemimah, the name of the second Keziah and the name of the third Keren-Happuch.*
>
> *In all the land were found no women so beautiful as the daughters of Job; and their father gave them an inheritance among their brothers.*
>
> *After this Job lived one hundred and forty years and saw his children and grandchildren for four generations.*
>
> *So, Job died, old and full of days.*   Job 42:12-17

Polycarp of Smyrna

Time after time, throughout the generations since the early Church, we see God tempering and transforming the faith of His people through the fires of adversity. It was the blazing flames of persecution that thrust the early Church into the purifying crucible, giving us martyrs like Polycarp whose awe-inspiring faith shone with holy radiance as flames licked his body.

Written about AD 156, within a year of the event it describes (AD 155), *The Martyrdom of Polycarp* is an authentic eyewitness report of the heroic death of an elderly man named Polycarp.[1]

---

[1] The Martyrdom of Polycarp. Letter from the Church of Smyrna to the Church at Philomelion in Phrygia. From Kirsopp Lake, The Apostolic Fathers, volume 2 (London: Heinemann, 1913). http://www.archive.org/details/apostolicfathers02lakeuoft

Polycarp was the bishop of Smyrna, today the city of Izmir, located on the west coast of Turkey.

Smyrna, is located in the Aegean Region of Turkey is a captivating blend of history, culture, and natural beauty. Known for its stunning coastlines, ancient ruins, and vibrant cities, this region is located near the turquoise waters of the Aegean Sea to the rolling hills dotted with olive groves.

Polycarp was part of the generation of church leaders who succeeded the apostles. He was taught by the Apostle John and was appointed to his office by the apostles themselves.

The account of Polycarp's death was written by the Christians of Smyrna, who wrote it as a letter and circulated it to all the churches. Polycarp's character and personal relationship with the Lord shone out in its simple words. The apparent defeat of his death became a triumphant witness to the resurrection.

Polycarp was martyred before the period of the great persecutions organized from Rome by emperors like Diocletian. His story reveals the tensions that were already building up throughout the empire, as Christians rejected the gods and goddesses that everyone else was worshipping. The pagans called the Christians "atheists" for this apparent lack of religious feeling. Polycarp made it clear to a Roman government official, that the real atheists are those who don't worship the one true God.

In the text, *The Martyrdom of Polycarp*, the local persecution of Christians was taking place. Some of Smyrna's Christians had already been put to death and search parties were looking for the bishop, who had been persuaded to do the prudent thing and leave town.

Someone tipped off the pursuers that Polycarp was hiding out at a farmhouse in the country.

The mounted police of Smyrna set out on Friday about suppertime. They carried their usual weapons, as if they were advancing against a bandit. Late in the evening, they arrived at the home of Polycarp to arrest him and found he was resting upstairs. He could have escaped to another place but decided to stay. "God's will be done," he said.

When Polycarp heard that the police were there, he went downstairs and talked with them. Everyone was amazed at his age and courage and wondered why there should be so much haste about arresting an old man like this. Despite the lateness of the hour, he had a table set for them to eat and drink, as much as they desired. He asked them to give him an hour to pray undisturbed and they agreed.

Polycarp stood and prayed out loud. He was so filled with the grace of God that, for two hours, he could not be silent. Those who listened were astounded and many were sorry that they had come to arrest such a venerable old man.

When Polycarp had finished his prayer, after remembering everyone who had ever crossed his path — both small and great, high and low — and the whole Church throughout the world, the time came for him to leave. They set him on an ass and led him into the city.

Save Yourself

The chief of police, named Herod, and his father, Niketas, met Polycarp there and took him into their carriage. Sitting beside him, they tried to persuade him to change his mind: "What harm is there in saying 'Lord Caesar' and offering sacrifice and saving yourself from death?"

At first Polycarp did not answer them, but when they kept at it, he said, "I am not going to do what you advise." Then they gave up trying to persuade him and began to make threats.

They forced him out of the carriage so fast that he scraped his shin getting out. Without even turning around, as though he had felt nothing, Polycarp walked on quickly and was taken to the noisy stadium.

As he entered, a voice from heaven came to him: "Be strong, Polycarp, and act like a man." No one saw the speaker, but our friends who were there heard the voice.

> *Be strong, Polycarp, and act like a man.*

No Fear

Polycarp was brought before the proconsul, who also tried to persuade him to deny his faith. "Respect your age," he said. "Swear by the divine power of Caesar. Change your mind. Say, 'Away with the atheists!'"

But Polycarp, with a solemn look at the unruly mob in the stadium, pointed to them and, looking up to heaven, said, "Away with the atheists!" The proconsul urged him harder. "Take the oath and I'll let you go. Curse Christ." However, Polycarp responded:

> "Eighty-six years I have served him, and he never did me any wrong," said Polycarp.
>
> "How can I blaspheme my King who saved me?"

When the proconsul kept insisting, "Swear by the divine power of Caesar," Polycarp answered, "If you vainly suppose that I will swear by the divine power of Caesar, as you say, and if you pretend that you do not know who I am, listen plainly: I am a Christian. And if you wish to learn the Christian message, arrange a meeting and give me a hearing."

"I have wild animals," the proconsul said. "I'll throw you to them unless you change your mind."

"Call them in," Polycarp replied, "for we are not allowed to change from something better to something worse."

Polycarp said, "You threaten with fire that burns for a short time and is soon quenched. You don't know about the fire of the coming judgment and eternal punishment that awaits the wicked. But why are you waiting? Come, do what you will."

Polycarp radiated courage and joy as he said these and many other things. Not only did his face show no sign of distress, it was so full of grace that the proconsul was astonished and sent his herald into the middle of the arena three times to announce:

> "Polycarp has declared that he is a Christian."

At the herald's announcement, the whole crowd roared with wild anger and a loud cry: "This is the father of the Christians, the destroyer of our gods, who teaches many to stop offering sacrifice to the gods."

Shouting out with one voice, they demanded that Polycarp be burned alive.

This happened incredibly fast — faster than it takes to tell the story. The mob hurried to gather wood and kindling from the shops and bathhouses. When the pyre was ready, Polycarp took off his outer clothes, unfastened his belt, and tried to take off his shoes.

Immediately they began to pile the wood around him. They were going to nail him to the stake as well, but Polycarp said, "Leave me the way I am. He who gives me power to endure the fire will help me to remain in the flames without moving, even without being secured by nails."

Polycarp put his hands behind him and was bound, like a noble ram out of a great flock ready for sacrifice, a burnt offering prepared and pleasing to God.

"Scorn the wild beasts and I'll have you burned alive, if you don't change your mind."

Looking up to heaven, he said:

> *Lord God Almighty, Father of your beloved and blessed Child, Jesus Christ, through whom we have received full knowledge of you, the God of angels and powers and of all creation, and of the whole family of the righteous, who live before you:*
>
> *I bless you for considering me worthy of this day and hour — of sharing with the martyrs in the cup of your Christ, so as to share in resurrection to everlasting life of soul and body in the Holy Spirit.*
>
> *May I be received among them into your presence today as a rich and acceptable sacrifice.*
>
> *For this, and for everything, I praise and glorify you through the eternal and heavenly high priest, Jesus Christ, your beloved Child. Through him and with him, may you be glorified with the Holy Spirit, both now and forever.*
>
> *Amen.*

When he had said the amen and finished his prayer, the men in charge of the fire lit it and a great flame blazed up. We who were given the privilege to witness it saw a great miracle and we have been kept alive so that we might report to others what happened.

The fire took the shape of a vaulted room, like a ship's sail filled with wind, and surrounded the body of the martyr like a wall. And he stood inside it — not as burning flesh, but as bread that is being baked, or as gold and silver being refined in a furnace.

And we smelled a fragrant aroma, like the scent of incense or other costly spices.

Seeing that his body could not be consumed by the fire, the lawless men finally commanded an executioner to go up and stab Polycarp with a dagger. When he did this, there came out a dove and so much blood that the fire was extinguished.

This indeed was one of God's chosen ones — the amazing martyr, Polycarp, an apostolic and prophetic teacher in our time, bishop of the Church in Smyrna. By his patient endurance he overcame the devil and gained the crown of immortality. Now he rejoices with the apostles and all the saints. He is glorifying God, the Father Almighty, and blessing our Lord Jesus Christ, the Savior and Captain of our souls and bodies, and the Shepherd of the Church throughout the world.

The Martyrdom of Polycarp could not Burn Him

When the Enemy saw the wonder of his martyrdom, his blameless life and now his crowning with immortality, he did his utmost to stop us keeping any memorial of him or taking possession of his holy body. He inspired Nicetes, the father of Herod, along with the Jews, to ask the governor not to hand over his body for burial. "They might turn from worshipping the crucified one," he said, "only to start worshipping this one."

They did not realize that it is impossible for us to abandon Christ who suffered for the salvation of the world, or to worship any other.

The centurion then, seeing the disturbance caused by the Jews, took the body and publicly burnt it. Later, we collected up his bones, more precious than jewels and better purified than gold, and put them in an appropriate place where, the Lord willing, we shall celebrate the birthday of his martyrdom each year with joy and rejoicing, both to remember those who have run their race and to prepare those yet to walk in their steps.

This is the story of the blessed Polycarp, the twelfth martyr in Smyrna, though he has a unique place memory of all people, being remembered even by all the heathen. He was not merely an illustrious teacher, but also a pre-eminent martyr, whose death all desire to imitate, being altogether consistent with the Gospel of Christ.

Having overcome the unjust governor with patience and acquired the crown of immortality, he now, with the apostles and all the righteous, glorifies God the Father with joy, and blesses our Lord Jesus Christ.

Will we resent the flames of adversity and curse the trial that threatens to undo us completely? Or will we trust our divine refiner to fulfill His purposes, surrendering ourselves to the painful but purposeful process of having our faith molten, melted, and transformed from impurity and weakness into a radiant expression of Christ's glory?

The choice is ours – to see our trials either as random tragedies to be endured, or intentional refiner's fires allowed by a good God to reveal genuine faith shining more brilliantly than precious metal refined by flames.

Indeed, the refining fires of affliction we face have the power to purify us from sin, selfishness, and superficial faith. When faithfully embraced, they temper us with perseverance, forge us with hope, and reveal the worth and radiance of a faith that endures. For the believer who surrenders to the process, trials transform us over the scorching flame into luminous examples of God's power and providence at work – precious souls of eternal, imperishable worth refined by the purposeful fires of a loving heavenly Father.

In the chapters ahead, we will examine what it looks like to trust the Refiner's process rather than shrink from it.

But first, let us reflect: what impurities in our own faith might God desire to burn away through trials? What areas of our lives have been clouded and tarnished, diminishing the radiance we are called to reflect?

The Refiner's fire has come to shape, mold and transform us into a faith of greater worth than gold – may we embrace its purifying work with open hearts and Kingdom perspective.

> *I will bring the one-third through the fire, will refine them as silver is refined, and test them as gold is tested.*
>
> *They will call on My name, and I will answer them. I will say, 'This is My people'; and each one will say, 'The LORD is my God.'*   Zechariah 13:9

The Crucible of Our Souls

Just as the refiner places the rough metal ore into a crucible to withstand the intense heat, so God allows His children to enter crucibles of affliction perfectly designed to test and purify our faith. Whether it is the crucible of a difficult relationship, the crucible of a chronic illness, or the crucible of emotional or spiritual crisis – each trial serves as a blistering furnace of refinement for our souls.

> *For You, O God, have tested us; You have refined us as silver is refined. You brought us into the net; You laid affliction on our backs.*
>
> *You have caused men to ride over our heads; We went through fire and through water; But You brought us out to rich fulfillment.*   Psalm 66:10-12

A crucible is a container in which metals or other substances may be melted or subjected to very high temperatures. Although crucibles have historically tended to be made out of clay, they can be made from any material that withstands temperatures high enough to melt or otherwise alter its contents.

The idea of the crucible holds deep spiritual significance. The crucible was originally a ceramic vessel used to separate pure elemental metals from impure ore and dross through extreme temperatures.

In the same way, the crucibles of suffering we experience are divine means of separating the pure faith within us from the impurities of sin, fear, pride and self-reliance that contaminate our walk with Christ.

Make no mistake – these crucibles are intensely uncomfortable places. The searing heat of the trial creates an inhospitable environment designed to radically reshape us from willing participants into humbled, purified, and transformed vessels reflecting Christ's glory. Yet it is crucial that we embrace the blessed, purposeful work of God's refining crucibles rather than resist their holy fires.

Embracing the Crucible

Too often, when the crucible of fiery trial appears, our first impulse is to escape it or pray for deliverance from it as quickly as possible. And, while God may occasionally provide an exit from our most intense sufferings, more frequently, He calls us to endure the crucible with faith and surrender, allowing the purifying work to be completed.

We see this pattern modelled by Christ himself, who "for the joy set before him endured the cross" (Hebrews 12:2), embracing the crucible of intense suffering for the greater purpose of God's redemptive plan. He knew the fires that tested him were part of God's sovereign design to purify a path of obedience all the way to death, even death on a cross (Philippians 2:8). In a similar way, the crucibles we face in this life are given by God to purify our faith and allegiance to Him alone through the refining process of adversity. We too must embrace the joy set before us, fixing our eyes on Jesus as the pioneer and perfecter of the faith He is shaping in us through trials.

> *Let this mind be in you which was also in Christ Jesus, who, being in the form of God, did not consider it robbery to be equal with God, but made Himself of no reputation, taking the form of a bondservant, and coming in the likeness of men. And being found in appearance as a man, He humbled Himself and became obedient to the point of death, even the death of the cross.*
>
> *Therefore, God also has highly exalted Him and given Him the name which is above every name, that at the name of Jesus every knee should bow, of those in heaven, and of those on earth, and of those under the earth, and that every tongue should confess that Jesus Christ is Lord, to the glory of God the Father.*
>
> *Philippians 2:5-11*

The prophet Isaiah provides further insight into the importance of faithfully enduring our crucibles of refinement: "See, I have refined you, though not as silver; I have tested you in the furnace of affliction" (Isaiah 48:10). We are reminded that embracing the furnace, though difficult, is by God's design for refining our faith to greater radiance, worth, and purity.

> *Behold, I have refined you, but not as silver. I have tested you in the furnace of affliction.* *Isaiah 48:10*

The Purifying Process

Like Shadrach, Meshach and Abednego, we may feel as though we have been thrown into the blazing furnace against our will at times (Daniel 3).

But we would be wise to consider their response - faithful in the face of the fiery crucible, without any attempt at escape or relief.

In so doing, Christ met them in the midst of the flames, refining and transforming their faith into a beacon that impacted an entire kingdom for God's glory. They embraced their crucible without compromise, emerging with radiant faith.

That must be our posture as well. For it is in the crucible where the purifying process unfolds, stripping away the worthless impurities that so often stain and cloud our witness.

Then Nebuchadnezzar was full of fury, and the expression on his face changed toward Shadrach, Meshach, and Abed-Nego. He spoke and commanded that they heat the furnace seven times more than it was usually heated. And he commanded certain mighty men of valour who were in his army to bind Shadrach, Meshach, and Abed-Nego, and cast them into the burning fiery furnace. Then these men were bound in their coats, their trousers, their turbans, and their other garments, and were cast into the midst of the burning fiery furnace.

Therefore, because the king's command was urgent, and the furnace exceedingly hot, the flame of the fire killed those men who took up Shadrach, Meshach, and Abed-Nego. And these three men, Shadrach, Meshach, and Abed-Nego, fell down bound into the midst of the burning fiery furnace.

Then King Nebuchadnezzar was astonished; and he rose in haste and spoke, saying to his counsellors, "Did we not cast three men bound into the midst of the fire?"

They answered and said to the king, "True, O king."

"Look!" he answered, "I see four men loose, walking in the midst of the fire; and they are not hurt, and the form of the fourth is like the Son of God."

Then Nebuchadnezzar went near the mouth of the burning fiery furnace and spoke, saying, "Shadrach, Meshach, and Abed-Nego, servants of the Most High God, come out, and come here." Then Shadrach, Meshach, and Abed-Nego came from the midst of the fire.

And the satraps, administrators, governors, and the king's counsellors gathered together, and they saw these men on whose bodies the fire had no power; the hair of their head was not singed nor were their garments affected, and the smell of fire was not on them.

Daniel 3:16-27

In the fired kiln of adversity:

- Our pride is melted away by trials that humble us
- Our selfishness is consumed by fires that teach sacrifice
- Our greed is incinerated by refining flames that expose vain idolatries
- Our impatience is scorched by long-suffering experiences
- Our doubts are forged into unshakeable confidence in God

It is through this holy refining process in the crucible, though intensely painful at times, that God smelts away our impurities as precious faith takes shape within us. Like refined silver and gold, we emerge steadfast, radiant, pure and able to clearly reflect the glory of our Redeemer to those around us.

> *The crucible is for silver and the furnace for gold, but the Lord tests the heart.*   *Proverbs 17:3*

So let us not merely endure the crucibles we face in this life, but wholeheartedly embrace them. For the fire is never without purpose or promise to those who entrust themselves to their divine Refiner. With Job, let our refining cry be:

> *He knows the way that I take; when He has tested me, I will come forth as gold.*   *Job 23:10*

The Necessity of Trials

When we think of what is required for spiritual growth and maturity in our Christian walk, we often envision things like devotional disciplines, biblical study, fellowship and service. While all of these are crucial elements, there is one catalyst for spiritual transformation that is unavoidable yet frequently resisted – the refining fire of trials and suffering.

From the very beginning in the garden of Eden, God's path for His children has involved difficulty, hardship and pain. Gen 3:16-19 makes it clear that suffering entered the human experience, as a consequence of sin, bringing with it the inevitable realities of relational strife, arduous toil and physical death.

A Necessary Refining

While suffering was never part of God's original intent, it nevertheless serves a vital redemptive purpose in the Christian's spiritual development and sanctification.

Paul declares in Romans:

> *Therefore, having been justified by faith, we have peace with God through our Lord Jesus Christ, through whom also we have access by faith into this grace in which we stand, and rejoice in hope of the glory of God.*
>
> *And not only that, but we also glory in tribulations, knowing that tribulation produces perseverance; and perseverance, character; and character, hope. Now hope does not disappoint, because the love of God has been poured out in our hearts by the Holy Spirit who was given to us.*
>
> *Romans 5:1-5*

This difficult yet necessary reality is woven throughout Scripture. God sent affliction and refining fire into the lives of countless biblical heroes to shape them according to His redemptive purposes:

- Joseph was sold into slavery and imprisoned to prepare him for leadership
- Moses spent 40 years exiled in the wilderness prior to liberation work
- David endured years running from Saul to shape his integrity as a future king
- Job passed through horrific calamity to transform his faith into childlike trust
- Paul's thorn in the flesh and imprisonments moulded him into a battle-tested witness

In each instance, the trials were severe, unrelenting flames that had the power to either destroy their faith completely or purify it into radiant, inextinguishable substance. The refining process was undoubtedly painful, undesired, and impossible to undergo in human strength alone. Yet it served as a divine catalyst for spiritual transformation and Kingdom impact none could have experienced without the crucible of affliction.

The Furnace of Transformation

Fire, heat, flame, crucible – the biblical imagery is unmistakable. The godly virtues of enduring faith, patience, and hope are not gently encouraged into existence, but purified and hardened through fiery trials that test their authenticity and core substance.

> *Behold, I have refined you, but not as silver; I have tested you in the furnace of affliction.* Isaiah 48:10

This truth beckons us to a profound paradigm shift regarding the difficulties and pains we encounter in this life. Rather than viewing them as random misfortunes, we must recognize them as intentional, divinely-ordained tools allowed by a loving Father for our spiritual growth and purification. In God's wise economy, trials fulfill powerful purposes:

- Burning away impurities of selfishness, greed, jealousy, idolatry that diminish our witness
- Exposing areas of weakness, vulnerability, pride and lack of faith that require shaping
- Forging resilient perseverance, godly character and everlasting hope within us
- Drawing us into deeper dependence on Christ as our only source of strength

While our natural inclination is to avoid adversity and embrace comfort at all costs, the path to genuine spiritual growth demands we surrender to the Master Refiner's purifying work. We must "not be conformed to this world," but embrace the trials and refining fire that transforms us by the "renewing of our minds".

> *And do not be conformed to this world, but be transformed by the renewing of your mind, that you may prove what is that good and acceptable and perfect will of God.*
>
> *Romans 12:2*

For just as the luminous, gleaming sword or brilliant, unbreakable diamond cannot take shape without being subjected to intense heat, friction and pressure – so our faith cannot radiate with spiritual vibrancy apart from persevering through divinely appointed furnaces of affliction. Though painful, these trials serve as God's purifying instruments to shape us into steadfast believers bearing stunning Christ-like character.

So let us neither resent nor despair over the seasons of blazing difficulty allowed into our lives. Instead, let us have kingdom perspective, recognizing each trial as an invitation to be stretched, strengthened, and shaped into radiant examples of our Savior's glorious image. For it is in surrendering to the refining work of affliction's flames that we come to experience the beauty of what fire produces - the priceless, imperishable substance of authentic, radiant, refined faith.

Here are some powerful examples from Scripture of biblical figures whose faith was dramatically strengthened through the refining fires of adversity.

Job

Few biblical stories illustrate the refining furnace of suffering more poignantly than that of Job. A man of upright character, Job faced a rapid succession of devastating trials - the loss of his children, wealth, health and standing all in terrible calamity. These were no mere inconveniences but a scorching blast furnace of affliction threatening to shipwreck his faith in God completely.

Yet God was purifying Job's half-faith into something radiant and unshakeable. The fires burned away false pretences, pride and fear until all that remained was simple childlike trust in the Almighty. Job's radiant resolve was to trust Him, exemplifying a transformation from misplaced self-righteousness to fully surrendered and refined faith.

> *Though He slay me, yet will I trust Him.*   *Job 13:15*

Joseph

The life of Joseph was a lengthy series of refining fires and trials. Sold into slavery by his brothers, he then endured false accusation and years of unjust imprisonment. These were sustained furnaces of adversity that could have produced bitterness, but instead forged Joseph's faith into resilience and perseverance.

By the time he was elevated to Pharoah's court, Joseph exhibited a refined character able to extend forgiveness and see God's hand at work through his afflictions. Rather than hardening his heart, the trials sharpened his receptivity to divine purposes – "You meant it for evil," he told his brothers, "but God intended it for good." Joseph's faith was strengthened to radiate unshakable confidence in the Refiner's plan.

> *Joseph said to them, "Do not be afraid, for am I in the place of God?*
>
> *But as for you, you meant evil against me; but God meant it for good, in order to bring it about as it is this day, to save many people alive.*
>
> *Genesis 50:19-20*

Moses

Even the man chosen to bring the Israelites out of bondage first had to endure his own furnace of adversity to prepare him. After being forced to flee Egypt as a refugee, Moses spent 40 wilderness years as a humble shepherd, a massive delay in his expected future. This season of adversity burned away Moses' self-reliance and pride, refining him into a mouldable instrument entrusted with bringing God's people out of slavery's oppression.

By the time God called him at the burning bush, Moses' initial arrogance had been replaced with a "Who am I?" humility – the necessary catalyst for fully depending on God's power and leading rather than his own. From being refined in Midian's crucible, Moses emerged as the meekest man on earth, wielding a purified faith able to confront Pharoah himself and bring about Israel's liberation.

> *But Moses said to God, "Who am I that I should go to Pharaoh, and that I should bring the children of Israel out of Egypt?"*   *Exodus 3:11*

Paul

Even the apostle Paul, whose gospel transformed the ancient world, was shaped through excruciating trials to have his faith refined. Having been spectacularly converted on the Damascus Road, Paul still faced persecutions, beatings, shipwreck, imprisonment, hunger and an afflicting "thorn in the flesh" which cultivated humility.

Rather than deterring his mission, these afflictions instilled in Paul a hardy, tempered faith able to endure literally anything. The furnace of adversity stripped away pride, fear and self-reliance until he could declare:

> *I have learned the secret of being content in any and every situation.*   *Philippians 4:12*

His was a radiant, refined faith formed through flames – giving him eternal perspective and unstoppable perseverance.

From Job to Joseph, Moses to Paul, the biblical pattern is consistent – God leverages trials and adversity as His chosen furnace for purifying and strengthening faith into radiant authenticity. What were meant as setbacks or defeats were divinely alchemized into spiritual refining. Adversity became the Refiner's tool for preparation, growth and forging enduring, imperishable trust in Him alone.

In seeing these transformations, we gain clarity that trials are not punishments, but loving provisions allowed by our heavenly Father to expose areas in need of refinement. The fiery process is harsh yet effective – intended to strip away pseudo-faith and self-reliance, replacing them with purified, rock-solid dependence on Christ alone.

These scriptural examples dare us to shift perspective on our own furnaces of affliction. Will we resent them as injustices or setbacks to be avoided? Or can we surrender to their purifying work, knowing that just like Job, Joseph, and Paul – we are being fashioned by the flames into radiant, steadfast witnesses revealing indelible faith in our Refiner and Redeemer?

Things Eternal

> *Therefore, we do not lose heart. Even though our outward man is perishing, yet the inward man is being renewed day by day.*
>
> *For our light affliction, which is but for a moment, is working for us a far more exceeding and eternal weight of glory, while we do not look at the things which are seen, but at the things which are not seen.*
>
> *For the things which are seen are temporary, but the things which are not seen are eternal.*
>
> *2 Corinthians 4:16-18*

Chapter 3: Trusting the Process

While understanding the divine purpose behind the refiner's fire is crucial, simply knowing why we face trials is not enough. We must come to a place of surrendering our lives and circumstances fully to God's purifying work, rather than railing and raging against the adversity that aims to shape us.

All too often, our first instinct when the fires of affliction arise is one of rebellion. We protest the pain, despair over our circumstances, and angrily question why a good God would allow such difficulty to enter our lives. In the midst of sickness, loss, injustice or persecution, we can easily become like Job's wife, who advised her husband to simply "Curse God and die!" (Job 2:9) rather than endure any further agony at the hands of the Refiner.

But bitter railing against our trials is the exact opposite of the surrendered perspective Scripture calls us to. Instead of kicking and screaming against the purifying work God intends, we are exhorted by the Apostle Peter to:

> *Therefore, humble yourselves under the mighty hand of God, that He may exalt you in due time, casting all your care upon Him, for He cares for you.*
> *Be sober, be vigilant; because your adversary the devil walks about like a roaring lion, seeking whom he may devour. Resist him, steadfast in the faith, knowing that the same sufferings are experienced by your brotherhood in the world.*
> *But may the God of all grace, who called us to His eternal glory by Christ Jesus, after you have suffered a while, perfect, establish, strengthen, and settle you. To Him be the glory and the dominion forever and ever. Amen.*
> 1 Peter 5:6-11

Surrendering to the refining process requires a fundamental humility that rests in God's higher purposes even when the fires of suffering rage fiercely around us.

The Choice to Surrender

In the crucible of trials, we are faced with a critical choice – will we resist the refining fires, or will we surrender ourselves in obedient humility to our Father's purifying work? The path of resistance only leads to greater anguish, bitterness, and despair as we foolishly fight against what God has ordained. The road of surrender ushers in profound peace, perspective, and unshakeable hope even in the midst of blazing trials.

We see this surrendered mindset modelled by Christ himself in the Garden of Gethsemane. Facing unfathomable agony on the cross, Jesus cried out "My Father, if it is possible, let this cup pass from me. Yet not my will but yours be done" (Luke 22:42).

Even the perfect Son of God felt the weight of the furnace He was entering. Yet He chose to surrender to the Refiner's purifying work - for the joy set before Him, He "endured the cross, scorning its shame."

> *Therefore we also, since we are surrounded by so great a cloud of witnesses, let us lay aside every weight, and the sin which so easily ensnares us, and let us run with endurance the race that is set before us, looking unto Jesus, the author and finisher of our faith, who for the joy that was set before Him endured the cross, despising the shame, and has sat down at the right hand of the throne of God.*
>
> *Hebrews 12:1-2*

Following our Saviour's example, surrendering to the refiner's fires is a matter of the heart, will and mind. It requires us to:

- Humble our hearts before the Refiner, submitting to His purposes
- Choose to align our wills with His, even when it means walking through flames
- Bring our minds into redemptive perspective, fixing our eyes on eternity

When faced with the crucible of adversity, our battle begins within before it can be waged against exterior trials.

We must take every thought captive under Christ's Lordship (2 Cor 10:5) and lay down our self-reliance, pride, anger and fear at the feet of the One who has allowed and overcome the refining fires we face.

> *For the weapons of our warfare are not carnal but mighty in God for pulling down strongholds, casting down arguments and every high thing that exalts itself against the knowledge of God, bringing every thought into captivity to the obedience of Christ, and being ready to punish all disobedience when your obedience is fulfilled.*
>
> *2 Corinthians 10:4-6*

The Blessing of Surrender

When we choose to surrender ourselves fully to the Refiner's work, assenting to His purifying process, rather than fighting against it, life-changing blessing awaits. As we lay down our self-efforts to douse the flames, God's Spirit flows unhindered allowing His purposes to unfold. No longer are we pitting our finite, temporal attempts against His infinite wisdom and view of eternity, but gladly entrusting ourselves to the loving hand that guides us through the furnace of transformation.

With an attitude of surrender, the fires that once felt destructive are revealed as purposeful tools in the hands of our heavenly Father. The very trials that threatened to undo us become molding experiences of redemption, revealing grit, resilience and a faith more precious than perishable gold.

Yes, the flames will still burn and affliction will sting for a season. Nowhere are we promised a life free from tears, pain and difficulty. But for those who surrender their lives as living sacrifices to the Master Refiner, peace reigns even in the midst of fiery furnaces.

Surrendered hearts find blessed relief, trading the despair of self-reliance for a lightness of being under Christ's easy yoke and burden.

> *Come to Me, all you who labour and are heavy laden, and I will give you rest. Take My yoke upon you and learn from Me, for I am gentle and lowly in heart, and you will find rest for your souls. For My yoke is easy and My burden is light.*
> *Matthew 11:28-30*

The refining process is experienced with God's joyful strength as our help and stay. What was once impossible to bear alone becomes possible through a total surrender of our lives. Like the Israelites once enslaved in Egypt, "their burden is lifted from their shoulders" (Psalm 81:3-6).

So let us choose to humbly surrender to the purifying work of the Refiner rather than stubbornly resisting His wise plans. With open hands and humble hearts, let us embrace the transformative fires He has allowed into our lives to shape us. For in doing so, we will emerge from the flames transformed and radiant - our faith revealed as that which cannot be destroyed, but only purified to shine ever more brilliantly for His glory.

> *We also rejoice in our sufferings, because we know that suffering produces perseverance; perseverance, character; and character, hope.*
> *Romans 5:3-4*

Having seen how God purposefully uses trials as a refining fire to purify our faith, we must next wrestle with what it looks like to actually trust Him in the process. For it is one thing to understand the divine refiner's purpose for subjecting our faith to scorching flames, but quite another to willingly surrender ourselves to His purifying work in the midst of adversity.

Our natural human instinct is to avoid pain and suffering at all costs. We bristle at the idea of enduring unnecessary hardship, seeking ease, comfort and healing at the first sign of the refiner's fire burning in our lives. Yet as we examine Scripture, over and over we see God's people called to do something paradoxical – to embrace suffering, persevere through it, and allow the purifying work to be accomplished.

Facing Fiery Trials with Joy

When we encounter the unavoidable crucibles and trials of life, our response is critically important. Do we respond with grumbling, bitterness and resentment toward the refining process? Or can we adopt the apostle James' mindset?

> *My brethren, count it all joy when you fall into various trials, knowing that the testing of your faith produces patience. But let patience have its perfect work, that you may be perfect and complete, lacking nothing.*
>
> *If any of you lacks wisdom, let him ask of God, who gives to all liberally and without reproach, and it will be given to him. But let him ask in faith, with no doubting, for he who doubts is like a wave of the sea driven and tossed by the wind.*
>
> *For let not that man suppose that he will receive anything from the Lord; he is a double-minded man, unstable in all his ways.*
>
> *James 1:2-8*

Such a disposition runs completely counter to our nature, which seeks to escape the refiner's fire at all costs. Yet James understood that the testing and shaping of genuine faith happens in the crucible of adversity.

Rather than vilify or resist the trials we face, we are called to lean into them with joyous trust, knowing that God the refiner is accomplishing something beautiful and eternal – the tempering of perseverance and steadfast character that produces a radiant hope.

Persevering In the Fire

Paul echoes this perspective in his letter to the Romans, encouraging believers to "rejoice in our sufferings," because the refining process produces perseverance, character and hope. Perseverance flows from embracing the refining fire rather than bailing at the first flicker of pain. It's the determination to remain steadfast under trial, confidence that God's purifying work will be accomplished if we simply trust the process.

Here we find great inspiration from the resilience modelled by Christ himself, who "for the joy set before him endured the cross, scorning its shame..." (Hebrews 12:2). Jesus' joy was rooted not in the suffering itself, but in the eternal weight of glory it would produce. In the same way, we are called to an eternal perspective, rejoicing in our afflictions as tools mightily used by God to chisel perseverance and enduring hope within us.

Far too often, we mistake God's refining process as a punishment. We view the trials in our life as cosmic consequences for our disobedience or lack of faith. Yet the opposite is true – God's pruning and shaping work in our lives is an expression of His love for us as a perfect Father.

Just as a loving parent disciplines their child through to build godly character and wisdom, so our heavenly Father's refining fires are an act of loving discipline to produce enduring faith and transformed lives that radiate His glory.

> *My son, do not despise the chastening of the LORD, nor be discouraged when you are rebuked by Him;*
>
> *For whom the LORD loves, He chastens and scourges every son whom He receives.*   *Hebrews 12:5-6*

The Blessing of Perseverance

What is the blessing produced by faithfully persevering through the fires of adversity rather than shrinking from them? The beautiful answer is that doing so forges unshakeable hope rooted in Christ. In the life of the believer who perseveres under trial, spiritual virtues become galvanized over the scorching flame. Genuine faith emerges from the refiner's fire shining with the radiance of:

- Steadfastness that cannot be rattled
- Patience anchored in the certainty of God's timing and work
- A hopeful confidence that transcends temporal suffering
- Uncompromised character marked by integrity and Christlikeness

With the purifying flame allowing these qualities to take shape, the believer finds their faith fortified, steadfast and able to endure any "trial of their faith, being much more precious than gold that perishes" (1 Peter 1:7).

In the face of whatever this life brings, they can hold fast to the "holy hope" modelled by the heroes of Scripture who "persevered because they saw what had been promised."

> *Now faith is the substance of things hoped for, the evidence of things not seen. For by it the elders obtained a good testimony.*
>
> *By faith we understand that the worlds were framed by the word of God, so that the things which are seen were not made of things which are visible.*   *Hebrews 11:1-2*

The cyclical pattern becomes transformative: The more we persevere through fiery trials, the more radiant and steadfast our hope becomes. The more unshakeable our hope, the greater our ability to persevere through the refiner's fires yet to come. It's a virtuous cycle of refining where God's people become "...overcomers through the blood of the Lamb and the word of their testimony."

> *And they overcame him by the blood of the Lamb and by the word of their testimony, and they did not love their lives to the death.*   *Revelations 12:11*

Far from something to be resisted or avoided, the divinely appointed trials and adversities we face, as followers of Christ, are intended to produce a supernatural perseverance and hope within us. When we learn to trust the purifying process, rather than escape it, an otherworldly resilience takes shape. A refining fire within is stoked, allowing our faith to blaze more brilliantly than ever before.

So how will we respond when the flames of adversity rise? Will we resist the refiner's merciful fire, angrily trying to douse it in bitterness and worry? Or will we surrender ourselves to the process willingly, allowing God to complete His purifying, shaping work in us? Regardless of the nature of the trial, the path to persevering hope requires trust - trusting our loving Father to accomplish His eternal purposes through these temporal trials. For it is this steadfast joyful trust that allows the refiner's flame to accomplish its work, smelting faith into something imperishable and radiant for His glory.

An Eternal Perspective

As we surrender to the refiner's purifying work in our lives, we must keep an eternal viewpoint fixed in our minds and hearts. For the trials and afflictions we encounter, though immensely painful in the present, are actually "light and momentary troubles" when compared to the immeasurable weight of glory that awaits.

> *Therefore, we do not lose heart. Even though our outward man is perishing, yet the inward man is being renewed day by day.*
>
> *For our light affliction, which is but for a moment, is working for us a far more exceeding and eternal weight of glory, while we do not look at the things which are seen, but at the things which are not seen.*
>
> *For the things which are seen are temporary, but the things which are not seen are eternal.*
>
> 2 Corinthians 4:16-18

It is all too easy to become consumed and overwhelmed by our current difficulties. The anguish of a tragic loss, the relentlessness of chronic illness or the oppression of injustice – these feel like anything but "light and momentary," when we are in the thick of suffering. Our limited human perspective binds us to the temporary pains of this life, blinding us to the eternal reality of what lies ahead.

Paul, however, reminds us to lift our eyes to the unseen, everlasting promise that utterly outstrips and outlasts our present trials.

An Eternal Weight of Glory

What is this eternal weight of glory to which Paul points our gaze?

It is nothing less than the promise of restored wholeness in Christ - the future reality of reigning with Him in the new heavens and new earth, free from every tear, every pain, every limit of our fallen existence (Rev 21:1-4). It is the radiant hope of eternity in glorified perfection, offering a weight of glory that transcends the temporal scale of our brief afflictions.

This incredible promise gives us resilience to not only endure the refiner's fires, but to "rejoice in our sufferings" (Rom 5:3) no matter how intense, knowing they are shaping us for greater measures of eternal glory and Christlike character. Our temporal perspective is realigned to the unstoppable reality that "our light and momentary troubles are achieving for us an eternal glory that far outweighs them all."

With the brilliance of Christ's own glory awaiting us, every trial takes on new purpose. The cancer diagnosis is rendered light as we await glorified bodies. The injustice suffered is momentary compared to the coming righteousness of His reign. The relational heartbreak passes in a blinding revelation of perfect wholeness to come. No flame of adversity, no refining furnace can extinguish the radiant promise of eternity.

Now I saw a new heaven and a new earth, for the first heaven and the first earth had passed away. Also, there was no more sea. Then I, John, saw the holy city, New Jerusalem, coming down out of heaven from God, prepared as a bride adorned for her husband. And I heard a loud voice from heaven saying,

"Behold, the tabernacle of God is with men, and He will dwell with them, and they shall be His people. God Himself will be with them and be their God. And God will wipe away every tear from their eyes; there shall be no more death, nor sorrow, nor crying. There shall be no more pain, for the former things have passed away."

Revelation 21:1-4

Therefore, having been justified by faith, we have peace with God through our Lord Jesus Christ, through whom also we have access by faith into this grace in which we stand, and rejoice in hope of the glory of God.

And not only that, but we also glory in tribulations, knowing that tribulation produces perseverance; and perseverance, character; and character, hope.

Now hope does not disappoint, because the love of God has been poured out in our hearts by the Holy Spirit who was given to us.

Romans 5:1-5

Chapter 4: The Purifying Flame

> *He will sit as a refiner and purifier of silver; He will purify the Levites and refine them like gold and silver.*
>
> *Malachi 3:3*

God's intention for allowing the furnace of affliction in our lives is not hardship for hardship's sake. No, the trials and adversities we face as His beloved children serve a very specific redemptive purpose - the purification of our faith until it gleams with radiant authenticity. Just as fire purges the impurities from precious metal ore, so the flames of suffering are designed to burn away the imperfections and contaminating elements from our walk with Christ.

This purifying process may feel harsh, painful, and even destructive in the moment. Yet like cancer radiation, the temporary anguish has eternal healing in mind. What feels like our spiritual undoing from a finite view is actually the heavenly refiner performing His skilled work – separating out the poor alloys that taint and dull our faith's radiance, while leaving behind sterling substance that radiates the transforming power of His grace.

Put another way, trials expose what our faith is truly anchored to. Is it secured only to the shifting sands of idols, temporal treasures and self-preservation? When affliction's winds and waves come crashing down, those fragile foundations are swept away.

For the believer, who is anchored in Christ the solid rock, the furnace serves to destroy any corrupting areas of misplaced allegiance, forging their faith into steadfast purity and radiance by fire.

This purifying flame burns on two fronts – the fires of sanctification expose our sin and self-effort to be consumed, while the fires of suffering eradicate any remaining idols, lies and false trusts. God in His patient mercy uses every method and technique to purify us from all that hinders love for Him.

The fires, though unpleasant, produce radiant beauty from the ashes.

Areas the Purifying Fire Exposes

1. Human Pride

From the beginning, pride has been the root corruption degrading our relationship with God. First issuing from Satan's desire to be like the Most High, pride triggered humanity's fall as we elevated ourselves to usurp God's rightful place. Unchecked, this inborn pride metastasizes into arrogance, self-reliance, envy, control and idolatry that displaces God from His throne over our hearts.

Yet the purifying flame of affliction has the power to utterly incinerate our pride. When we face trials beyond our ability to power through or control, our self-sufficiency and pride in abilities is exposed as futile. Hardship burns away the illusion that we can be masters of our own fate apart from Christ. It is then, in our desperate helplessness, that God's grace and power are allowed to blaze forth as our only means of enduring the furnace victoriously.

For the prideful person, the fires of adversity become an unwelcomed purifying agent – shaping humility, dependence and childlike trust in God, rather than self. Like a proud King Nebuchadnezzar driven to humiliating insanity until he learned to glorify God (Daniel 4), the furnace of affliction scorches away our pride until we are reduced to utter reliance on the Refiner's deliverance.

What was once inflated pride and arrogance is replaced by humble, radiant faith that finds its strength in God alone.

> *At the end of the twelve months, he was walking about the royal palace of Babylon. The king spoke, saying, "Is not this great Babylon, that I have built for a royal dwelling by my mighty power and for the honour of my majesty?" While the word was still in the king's mouth, a voice fell from heaven:*
>
> *"King Nebuchadnezzar, to you it is spoken: the kingdom has departed from you! And they shall drive you from men, and your dwelling shall be with the beasts of the field. They shall make you eat grass like oxen; and seven times shall pass over you, until you know that the Most High rules in the kingdom of men and gives it to whomever He chooses."*
>
> *That very hour the word was fulfilled concerning Nebuchadnezzar; he was driven from men and ate grass like oxen; his body was wet with the dew of heaven till his hair had grown like eagles' feathers and his nails like birds' claws.*
>
> *Daniel 4:29-33*

2. Idolatrous Attachments

No matter how well-disguised, our hearts are always in pursuit of creating counterfeit idols to displace God's rightful supremacy. Whether it be career success, financial security, our families, or our physical bodies, we all have deep tendencies to obsessively fix our identities and hopes on earthly attachments apart from Christ.

The purifying fire of affliction burns these idolatrous loves until, like Abraham having to sacrifice Isaac, they no longer compete with God's rightful Lordship over us.

Sudden unemployment reduces the career idol to ash. Failing health destroys the bodily idol we chased and polished. Family strife topples domestic idols off their pedestals. In their place, the refiners fire purifies our gaze until only Christ radiates as our magnificent obsession and great reward.

Job illustrated this refining process powerfully as the fires of overwhelming loss stripped him of possessions, family, health – everything he was secretly putting hope in, apart from God. Through the purging fire he declared in humility, "Naked I came from my mother's womb, and naked I will depart. The LORD gave and the LORD has taken away; may the name of the LORD be praised."

> *Then Job arose, tore his robe, and shaved his head; and he fell to the ground and worshiped. And he said:*
>
> *"Naked I came from my mother's womb and naked shall I return there. The Lord gave, and the Lord has taken away; Blessed be the name of the Lord."*
>
> *In all this, Job did not sin nor charge God with wrong.*
>
> *Job 1:20-22*

Only Job's faith in the Refiner remained, a radiant and purified trust that could then proclaim with authenticity, "Though He slay me, yet will I hope in him." The fires burned away all transient idols until only the eternal worship of God was left pure and undefiled.

Similarly, in our lives, the furnace lays bare the half-hearted faith that tries to keep one foot in the world's attachments and one in the Kingdom. The purifying flame tests the substance of our allegiance, exposing what we covertly cling to in place of wholehearted abandon to Christ. However, are we willing to let our most cherished earthly idols be stripped away, surrendering to the Refiner's work no matter the cost?

When allowed to accomplish its purpose, the fire banishes our idolatry, leaving only radiant undivided love for our one true prize – Christ Himself.

3. *Sinful Habits and Self-Reliance*

The purifying flame of trials also exposes besetting sins, weaknesses and self-reliant patterns that quench the Spirit's work. Like lifting the lid on a neglected chimney to let the air flow freely, the adversities and afflictions of life lay bare the accumulated soot defiling and stifling our faith.

Whether it's enslavement to lust, greed, anger, addictions, or simply a lack of abiding prayer, the purifying fires allowed into our lives by God's grace have the power to quite literally burn away the binding chains of our sin. They expose the flimsy self-remedies we use to try and compensate for or cover up these deficiencies.

When affliction strips us bare, with no recourse but crying out to God, we are offered a profound choice – cling to our paltry efforts at self-redemption or radical surrender and throw ourselves on the blazing mercies of the one true Redeemer.

David, the man after God's own heart, expressed this tension:

> *There is no soundness in my flesh because of your indignation; there is no health in my bones because of my sin.*
> *Psalm 38:3*

David's personal refining fire came as family chaos, guilt, and rebellion from his catastrophic fall. Yet this purifying affliction uncovered the hidden rottenness in his soul that he could no longer ignore or compensate for alone. Crushed under the weight of his iniquity and God's righteous refining work, David radiated a purified and renewed heart by crying out:

> *Create in me a clean heart, O God, and renew a steadfast spirit within me.*
>
> *Do not cast me away from Your presence, and do not take Your Holy Spirit from me.*   *Psalm 51:10-11*

His transparent humility and surrender as a broken sinner in need of God's unconditional grace and refining fire produced radiant authenticity.

In seasons of refining fire trials, we are granted the same mercy - our besetting sins and efforts at self-salvation are exposed as impotent, unable to bear the scorching furnace we face. Clinging to our defiant self-reliance would only lead to spiritual ruin. But by throwing ourselves in full desperation on God our only Redeemer, we are purified and revived with renewed purity and faith to carry us through any tribulation.

Jesus proclaimed:

> *Blessed are the pure in heart, for they shall see God.*
> *Matthew 5:8*

The purifying fires God allows into our lives become blessings in disguise – ruthless agents wielding divine power to incinerate all impurities clouding our spiritual eyesight from seeing Him clearly. Refining fire removes the obstructions of pride, idolatrous attachment and sinful habits that choke our radiance.

From the ashes of our striving emerges authentic faith no longer hindered by self-reliance, but abounding with liberating dependence on Christ, our All in All.

Learning to cling to Christ alone as our firm foundation

As the purifying flames of adversity do their radical work, burning away pride, idols and self-reliant strivings, we are left with a precious revelation – Christ alone is our firm, unshakable foundation on which to build our lives. Until the fires remove all other fragile foundations and false trusts, we cannot truly cling to the Solid Rock with unwavering grip.

Scripture beckons us to make Christ our singular foundation from the outset:

> *For no one can lay any foundation other than the one already laid, which is Jesus Christ.*   *1 Cor. 3:11*

Yet our human tendency is to construct complex scaffolding around this foundation, anchoring portions of our identity, worth and security to temporal sources – our careers, relationships, accomplishments, bank accounts, appearance and so on. While not innately evil, these become corrupted foundations when we displace Christ as our primary basis and build our lives upon them.

This is where the refining fire proves immensely merciful, even when it feels catastrophic in the moment. The very unravelling of relationships, loss of jobs, depletion of resources and crumbling of status is God's severe grace at work. With surgical precision, He is stripping away every other fragile foundation we have tried to build on until only Jesus Christ remains.

The fires are purging our lives of false securities and idolatrous attachments so that our full desperation and dependence can rest uncompromisingly upon Him.

The Radiance of God-Sufficiency

When every other foothold and foundation has been consumed by the refining flame, those who endure the process are offered an incredible vista – the breathtaking radiance and sufficiency of Christ as their unshakable Rock of refuge. Having surrendered all other vain foundations, they now find themselves fully planted upon and satisfied in Him alone.

This purifying work was poignantly displayed through the Apostle Paul's "thorn in the flesh" – a chronic tormentor allowed by God to keep him securely rooted in Christ rather than self-reliance. Three times Paul pleaded for it to be removed like a soldier asking to be relieved of brutal orders.

Yet God's response was crystal clear:

> *He said to me, "My grace is sufficient for you, for My strength is made perfect in weakness." Therefore, most gladly I will rather boast in my infirmities, that the power of Christ may rest upon me.*
>
> *Therefore, I take pleasure in infirmities, in reproaches, in needs, in persecutions, in distresses, for Christ's sake. For when I am weak, then I am strong.*
>
> *2 Corinthians 12:9-10*

In the crucible of that relentless affliction, Paul's self-sufficiency was steadily consumed until all he had left was to embrace radical dependence on God's sufficient grace. And in doing so, he came to radiate with the very power of Christ Himself.

This is the purified radiance that emerges from the furnace of affliction - the blazing revelation of God's incomparable, inexhaustible sufficiency to uphold, sustain and empower those who have relinquished every other foundation and pretence. In our striving self-reliance before trials, we could only eke out dimly lit displays of the Christian life, powered by our finite efforts. Once the furnace has rendered us poured-out empty before God, the unrelenting Flame of His presence rushes in to cloistered souls in brilliant, all-sufficient power.

Anchored to the Unshakeable

With the purifying fire burning away all other pitiful foundations, what remains is an anchor moored to the Unshakable. Paul spoke about the crushing in his exhortation to the Corinthian church.

> *We are hard pressed on every side, but not crushed; perplexed but not in despair; persecuted but not abandoned; struck down but not destroyed.*
>
> *2 Corinthians 4:8-9*

This childlike, fiery radiance cannot be extinguished, because it is upheld by Christ's immovable sufficiency, not our own strategies and self-strivings.

It is this revelatory perspective that Isaiah to proclaim with blazing flare:

> *Though the mountains be shaken and the hills removed, yet my unfailing love for you will not be shaken.   Isaiah 54:10*

When all other foundations are purged away by refining flames, God's steadfast love and sufficiency alone remain.

This is the radiant cry of those purified by the refiner's fire – we have nothing left but Christ and the revelling assurance that He is more than enough! Even when mountains crumble away under the weight of affliction, we cannot be abandoned or undone because we are anchored to the Unshakable One whose grace and loving-kindness are the solitary, inexhaustible reality upon which we are sustained.

In the end, every raging trial that strips us of all other earthly foundations and forces us to hold fast to Christ alone is a brutal mercy. For those who endure the purifying process, it forges a radiance that cannot be replicated without the furnace's work – simple, purified, childlike clinging to Jesus as our all-sufficient Rock, Redeemer and Reward, no matter what flames flicker all around. By His grace the refining fire burns away every lesser thing until our hearts, steadied and radiant, cry out with joyous desperation

> *You are my portion and my cup of blessing. You guard all that is mine!*   Psalm 16:5

The Sustaining Joy of His Presence

As followers of Christ, we are called to something paradoxical - to experience profound joy and contentment in the midst of affliction's furnace. While our natural instinct is to angrily rail against adversity or despair under its weight, Scripture beckons us to an entirely different counter-intuitive posture. We are summoned to find our satisfaction and rejoicing not in favourable circumstances, but in the all-sufficient presence of God Himself, especially when engulfed by refining fires.

This is the supernatural perspective modelled by the Apostles after being flogged for preaching Christ:

> *They left the presence of the council, rejoicing that they were counted worthy to suffer dishonour for the Name.* Acts 5:41

How could they find delight in the midst of persecution's agony? Their joy was rooted not in their situation but in the transcendent Presence that accompanied and vindicated their suffering for the gospel.

Christ's nearness outshone and overwhelmed the temporal pains they endured.

The prophet Habakkuk expressed a similar unshakeable joy - not in desirable conditions, but in the covenantal God who remains faithful despite any circumstance:

> *Though the fig tree may not blossom, nor fruit be on the vines; Though the labour of the olive may fail, and the fields yield no food;*
>
> *Though the flock may be cut off from the fold, And there be no herd in the stalls — Yet I will rejoice in the Lord, I will joy in the God of my salvation.*   Habakkuk 3:17-18

In the throes of famine and want, Habakkuk modelled a radiant contentment found not in provision or ease, but in the beauties of the Divine Presence alone. This is the blazing secret to maintaining joy in the refiner's furnace.

The Nearness That Sustains

To find our sufficiency in God's presence during trials is not an ethereal, ungrounded platitude. It is a supernatural truth that the eternal Creator has drawn near to us in the most intimate way imaginable through Christ's incarnation. "The Word became flesh and made his dwelling among us" (John 1:14), so that in our afflictions we would never be abandoned or alone, but could draw sustaining joy from the reality of Emmanuel – God with us.

It is Christ's abiding presence that allows Paul to proclaim, "I have learned the secret of being content in any and every situation" (Phil. 4:12). That secret was not some life-hacking technique, but the revelation that no matter how harsh the circumstance, he was never severed from the all-satisfying "Bread of Life" Himself who proclaimed: "I am the bread of life. Whoever comes to me will never go hungry" (John 6:35). In prison, shipwrecked, flogged or fleeing – Paul's vibrant joy in those darkest furnaces flowed from feasting on the inextinguishable presence of Christ.

Like the Hebrew believers in Egypt before the Exodus, those who have been joined to Jesus through His redeeming work experience glorious, counterintuitive provision in the wastelands:

> *He gave them bread from heaven to satisfy them.*
>
> *Psalm 105:40*

Though surrounded by barren scarcity, they receive divine manna – eternal provision for their souls directly from God's hand. It is this heavenly bread, this transcendent Presence alone that fully satisfies the hungry soul when all other supports and provisions have been stripped away by fiery trials.

Clinging to His Word

While Christ's presence is readily accessible in suffering, we must train our gaze to apprehend it. And there is no better resource for this than feasting on His Word as our sustaining manna when furnaces rage.

> *Your words were found, and I ate them, and Your word became to me the joy and rejoicing of my heart.*
>
> *Jeremiah 15:16*

When all temporal foundations for joy have been stripped away by the refining process, God's Word alone remains as our indestructible source of life, nourishment and gladness.

> *I have calmed and quieted my soul like a weaned child with its mother.* *Psalm 131:2*

To lean into this divine reality is to discover a contentment marked by rich, radiant joy - not an artificial happiness detached from sorrow, but a bedrock of purposeful and ceaseless celebration.

This rejoicing supersedes circumstance because it flows from an inextinguishable Source - the all-sufficient presence of God that delights the soul in any furnace or famine.

Like the three Hebrew youths in the fiery furnace, those who abide in God's comforting presence find sacred provision and unexplainable ecstasy amid the flames that should consume them. Their response to all who witnessed their radiant joy was simply:

> "Look!" he answered, "I see four men loose, walking in the midst of the fire; and they are not hurt, and the form of the fourth is like the Son of God." Daniel 3:25

For where Christ's presence dwells, supernatural delight reigns, no matter how intense the inferno blazes around it.

So, as we endure affliction's furnace, may we find our satisfaction not in comfort or ease, but in the all-satisfying presence of our Saviour Himself. When anxiety looms, let us feast on the Bread of Life. When depression overwhelms us, may we rejoice in God our Salvation.

And when our final hour grows dark, may we pass through that ultimate fiery trial cradled in Christ's eternal joy, echoing the radiant affirmation:

"God's presence is here; it is everything!"

Chapter 5: Emerging Refined

The refining fires of adversity, as harsh and scorching as they may feel, are always purposeful in the lives of believers. While our temporal perspective sees only pain and difficulty, an eternal lens reveals the divine process at work - God's merciful shaping of radiant, refined faith that brings Him praise at the unveiling of Jesus Christ.

> *These have come so that the proven genuineness of your faith — of greater worth than gold, which perishes even though refined by fire — may result in praise, glory and honour when Jesus Christ is revealed.* 1 Peter 1:7

Inevitably, affliction's furnace feels destructive, as if it will be the very undoing of our spiritual lives. Tears, anxiety, anger, confusion - we are overwhelmed by the intense heat threatening to consume us. Yet this is simply the illusion caused by our short-sighted human vision, unable to see the greater spiritual realities at work.

The truth is, those who endure the furnace's blaze with faith and surrender are not abandoned to be destroyed, but lovingly positioned to have their faith purified into an everlasting substance far more precious than gold. This radiant transformation is God's very aim in subjecting our faith to the refiner's flames. We emerge from furnaces of affliction hardened into imperishable gemstones reflecting the beauty of our Redeemer to the praise of His glory.

The Radiance of Tempered Faith

The faith forged by enduring the furnace is decisively distinct from the untested, fragile belief we started with before trials. It has been hammered, heated and moulded through adversity into something hardy and crystalline that cannot be marred or shattered by any temporal circumstance.

This tempered resilience stems from having our allegiances clarified and solidified under the scorching blaze. The fires have purged our spiritual dependencies - exposing areas of self-reliance, pride, idolatry and sin that previously stunted our growth. Like Paul, who declared "When I am weak, then I am strong," radiant believers are rendered helpless by the furnace, surrendering all self-sufficiency to cling to Christ alone.

But from this broken posture of total dependence, their faith emerges refined into something paradoxically powerful and dazzling bright. Having been stripped of all shaky foundations, their trust has become a singular focus fixed on God as immovable Rock, making them resilient and steadfast despite any shakings. With all self-efforts incinerated, Christ's indwelling power radiates unobscured through their emptied lives (2 Cor 4:7). The resultant faith is vibrant and bold, exhibiting rocklike perseverance and brave confidence in the face of any lingering heat from the refining process.

Dietrich Bonhoeffer

"When Christ calls a man, he bids him come and die."[2] "A Christian's secular vocation receives new recognition from the gospel only to the extent that it is carried on while following Jesus."

Dietrich Bonhoeffer (4 February 1906 – 9 April 1945) is one of the most-quoted Christian theologians of the last 100 years, inspiring generations of believers.

Dietrich Bonhoeffer was a German Lutheran pastor and anti-Nazi dissident who was a key founding member of the Confessing Church. His writings on Christianity's role in the secular world have become widely influential. His 1937 book *The Cost of Discipleship* is described as a modern classic.[1] This work is a profound exploration of what it means to follow Christ and the sacrifices that come with true discipleship. Bonhoeffer emphasized the concept of "costly grace," which contrasts with "cheap grace." The idea that grace is freely given, but requires no real commitment or change in one's life. The book challenged readers to live out their faith authentically and to embrace the demands of discipleship with courage and conviction.

Apart from his theological writings, Bonhoeffer was known for his staunch resistance to the Nazi dictatorship, including vocal opposition to Adolf Hitler's euthanasia program and the genocidal persecution of Jews.[2] He was arrested in April 1943 by the Gestapo and imprisoned at Tegel Prison for 1½ years. Later, he was transferred to Flossenbürg concentration camp.

---

[2] The Cost of Discipleship, 1959, page 11, by Dietrich Bonhoeffer.

Bonhoeffer was arrested by the Gestapo at his parents' home in Charlottenburg, Germany, in April 1943. He had broken many German laws by helping Jewish neighbours and by using his position as a government intelligence officer to evade service in the Nazi army. Bonhoeffer was jailed until October 1944 at Tegel Prison north of Berlin in relative comfort, allowing him the time and space to read and write prolifically for most of his imprisonment.[3]

After his participation in the now-famous Hitler assassination plot was exposed, Bonhoeffer was convicted of new crimes and was moved from Tegel to Prinz-Albrecht-Strasse, then to Buchenwald concentration camp, and finally to Flossenbürg, where he was hanged with six others on April 9, 1945, just one month before Germany's surrender to the Allied forces. Bonhoeffer's short life came to a premature end.

---

[3] Photo of Tegel Prison by Rafael Galejew,
https://commons.wikimedia.org/w/index.php?curid=100284974

On 21 April 1945, the Tegel Prison was dissolved and all inmates were released. The French occupation forces took over the prison in July 1945 and returned it to the German administration in October, which immediately put it back into operation.

Hardly any of us know the final result of our daily choices. And while many readers of Christian-living bestsellers love Bonhoeffer's wisdom about true satisfaction in *The Cost of Discipleship* and *Life Together*, we can only guess at how the theologian would evaluate his own life or his last days. Did he make the right choices?[4]

---

[4] Some of this information is sourced from Christianity Today. https://www.christianitytoday.com/2023/09/cost-of-creativity-bonhoeffer-set-aside-ethics-for-art-did/

Stations on the Way to Freedom[5]
by Dietrich Bonhoeffer

Discipline

If you set out to seek freedom, then you must learn, above all things, discipline of your soul and your senses, lest your desires and then your limbs perchance should lead you now hither, now yon.

Chaste be your spirit and body, subject to yourself completely, in obedience seeking the goal that is set for your spirit.

Only through discipline does one learn the secret of freedom.

Action

Not always doing and daring what's random, but seeking the right thing.

Hover not over the possible, but boldly reach for the real.

Not in escaping to thought, in action alone is found freedom.

Dare to quit anxious faltering and enter the storm of events, carried alone by your faith and by God's good commandments; then true freedom will come and embrace your spirit, rejoicing.

Suffering

Wondrous transformation. Your hands, strong and active, are fettered.

Powerless, alone, you see that an end is put to your action.

Yet now you breathe a sigh of relief and lay what is righteous, calmly and fearlessly into a mightier hand, contented.

Just for one blissful moment you could feel the sweet touch of freedom.

Then you gave it to God, that God might perfect it in glory.

---

[5] The Stations on the Road to Freedom were **written after the news of the failure of the attempt on Hitler's life in July 1944**, an event which must have convinced Bonhoeffer that his own end was near.

> ### *Death*
> Come now, highest of feasts on the way to freedom eternal, Death, lay down your ponderous chains and earthen enclosures walls that deceive our souls and fetter our mortal bodies, that we might at last behold what here we are hindered from seeing.
>
> Freedom, long have we sought you through discipline, action, and suffering. Dying, now we discern in the countenance of God, your own face.

Jan Huss

These are a few among a great cloud of witnesses (Hebrews 12:1) who invested their fleeting lives in the refining process until all impurities were burned away, leaving purified faith that could not be destroyed but only revealed in spectacular brilliance. It was this same purified faith that allowed martyrs like Jan Huss to declare with visionary hope while being burned at the stake:

> *I hope, by God's grace, that I am truly a Christian, not deviating from the faith, and that I would rather suffer the penalty of a terrible death than wish to affirm anything outside of the faith or transgress the commandments of our Lord Jesus Christ.*   *Jan Huss*

Jan Huss, sometimes anglicized as John Hus or John Huss, and referred to in historical texts as Iohannes Hus or Johannes Huss, was a Czech theologian and philosopher who became a Church reformer and the inspiration of Hussitism, a key predecessor to Protestantism, and a seminal figure in the Bohemian Reformation. Jan was born in 1369 AD in Husinec, Czechia and died 6 July 1415 AD (aged 46 years) in Konstanz, Germany.

Jan was a radiant, prophetic witness that pierced through the smoke – forged in the furnace yet shining in immortal splendour.[6] He was a Czech Church Reformer of the Catholic Church in Bohemia. Huss was opposed to the selling of indulgences and delivered an address regarding this in 1412.

---

[6] Jan Hus was a 15th Century Reformer who lived 1373-1415. His public address against indulgences *Quaestio magistri Johannis Hus de indulgentiis* was taken literally from the last chapter of Wycliffe's book, *De ecclesia*, and his treatise, *De absolutione a pena et culpa*.

Huss also opposed the right of the church to take up the sword. He also believed that the pope or bishop should pray for his enemies.

Shortly after arriving in Constance, he was arrested and placed in close confinement, from which he never emerged. Hus' enemies succeeded in having him tried before the Council of Constance as a Wycliffite heretic. All that the earnest intervention by the Bohemian nobles could obtain for him was three public hearings, at which he was allowed to defend himself and succeeded in refuting some of the charges against him.

The council urged Huss to recant in order to save his life, but to the majority of its members he was a dangerous heretic fit only for death. When he refused to recant, he was solemnly sentenced on July 6, 1415, and burned at the stake.

There has been much dispute over the extent to which Huss was indebted to Wycliffe for his theological beliefs. At the Council of Constance, he refused to submit to the council's demand that he disavow Wycliffe entirely, and he undoubtedly did support the doctrine of predestination and advocate the supremacy of biblical authority over that of the Catholic church. Huss's views can also be interpreted as the culmination of the Czech national reform movement, however. His followers and subsequent Bohemian religious reformers adopted the name Hussites.

During his exile in 1412-14, Huss substituted for his popular preaching in Prague a series of writings in Czech, and these have since become classics of Czech literature and are equally important in the history of the Czech language, because Huss developed a new and simpler orthography. The most important of these works is his popular tract *Vyklad viery, desatera a patere* ("Exposition of the Faith, of the Ten Commandments, and of the Lord's Prayer"). Huss' writings in Czech and Latin include other religious tracts, learned treatises and lectures, collections of his sermons, and personal letters.

On the following two pages, I have included two of Jan Huss' letters. These letters were written during his exile and imprisonment in 1537. They contain a preface by Martin Luther, were translated by Campbell Mackenzie and published by William Whyte & Co., Booksellers to the Queen Dowager in London in 1846.[7]

> I hope, by God's grace, that I am truly a Christian, not deviating from the faith, and that I would rather suffer the penalty of a terrible death than wish to affirm anything outside of the faith or transgress the commandments of our Lord Jesus Christ.
>
> John Hus

---

[7] https://en.wikisource.org/wiki/Letters_of_John_Huss_Written_During_His_Exile_and_Imprisonment

Dr Martin Luther wrote the following:

> *In order to render more prudent, and to instruct, by means of the tyrannical judgments of the Council of Constance, all theologians that may be hereafter called to sit in a council of the Roman Church.*
>
> *Should any man read these letters, or hear them read, being, at the same time, in possession of a sound intelligence, and, in the face of God, having a regard for his own conscience, he will not, I am convinced, hesitate to allow that John Huss was endowed with the precious gifts of the Holy Spirit.*
>
> *Observe, in fact, how firmly he clung, in his writings and his words, to the doctrines of Christ; with what courage he struggled against the agonies of death; with what patience and humility he suffered every indignity; and with what greatness of soul he at last confronted a cruel death in defence of the truth;—doing all these things alone and unaided, before an imposing assembly of the most powerful and eminent men, like a lamb in the midst of wolves and lions.*
>
> *If such a man is to be regarded as a heretic, no person under the sun can be looked on as a true Christian. By what fruits, then, shall we recognise the truth, if it is not manifest by those with which John Huss was so richly adorned?*

The Radiant Culmination

While trials feel chaotic and potentially ruinous, from the divine vantagepoint they are the skilful work of a Master Artisan sculpting us for nobility in His courts and preparing us to be revealed in blazing radiance when Christ returns. The furnace of affliction is allowed to do its arduous work for a singular purpose:

In that supreme moment, all who have entrusted themselves to the refiner's purifying process will be unveiled as immortal examples of transformed character, steadfast obedience and triumphant faith. Finally freed from the lingering effects of sin, the fullness of our redeemed radiance will be gloriously displayed. Eyes once clouded by sorrow's stinging smoke will be made brilliant by gazing on our precious Redeemer face to face. What was once temporal dross is eternally purged as we reflect His splendour from glory to ever-increasing glory.

While gold refined by fire perishes and fades, our faith – tested and forged in the furnace of affliction – will radiate with everlasting brilliance before our King. In that day, we will join the radiant multitude "robed in white, purified by the redeeming blood and refining fire, singing the triumphant song:

> *You are worthy, O Lord our God, to receive glory and honour and power. For you created everything, and it is for your pleasure that they existed and were created!*
>
> *Revelation 4:11*

Far from random pain, the trials permitted by our loving Father have been carefully orchestrated to produce a faith radiant for eternity. While we cannot see it in our temporal sufferings, every tear and tribulation has been filtered through the sovereign prism of His purposes as tools to melt, mold and purify our characters into resplendent reflections of Christ's beauty. When finally unveiled in His presence at last, we will thrill to see our emerald, ruby and diamond facets refracting our Savior's glories to those around the heavenly throne - the ultimate culmination of lives lived as loving submissions to the divine Refiner's care.

That poetic cry expresses so powerfully the longing to surrender ourselves fully to the refining fire and be purified for God's purposes. It echoes the words of the psalmist in Psalm 51:10: "Create in me a pure heart, O God, and renew a steadfast spirit within me."

When we embrace that holy desire to be purified like precious metal in the refiner's fire, we are positioning ourselves for profound spiritual transformation. The trials and sufferings we face are allowed by God's loving hand to do just that - to burn away the impurities, idols and sinful dross that contaminate our devotion.

As hard as it is, we must open ourselves up to that purifying process rather than resist it. Yielding to the refiner's fire with a heart that cries "I choose to be holy, set apart for You my Master" is an act of trusting God's higher purposes in our afflictions. It's an admission that we need that intense heat to deal with the sin and self-reliance that quench our spiritual radiance and fortitude.

When we embrace the painful reality that "I must be holy" rather than cling to our worldly comforts, we are positioned for incredible spiritual refinement. The very thing that once felt destructive – the "furnace of affliction" – becomes the indispensable catalyst purifying us for radiant, steadfast holiness.

So may that be our cry and heart's meditation in every season of fiery trial - "Purify me God, let me pass through the crucible so that I reflect Your brilliant holiness. Do whatever refining work is needed, for my soul's one desire is to be set apart for You and ready to do Your will, no matter the cost."

This is the road to having our faith forged into radiant, imperishable substance reflecting the holy light of our Savior. When we surrender to being stripped of impurities and remade in His purifying fire, our lives become fuelled by an internal holiness nothing can extinguish. Refined by God Himself, we emerge with transformed character tempered for eternal radiance and purpose.

Our brief years of earthly affliction and flame are accomplishing an exponential weight of glory. When the last ember has died and the smoke has cleared, only our refined radiance will remain - illuminated illustrations of Christ's praise for ages unending.

A Royal Priesthood

No trial is wasted for the Christian who entrusts their life to the divine refiner. As we embrace the difficult, but holy process of being refined by fire, our faith is transformed and strengthened to radiate the beauty and worth of Christ.

You are chosen people of God.

Every situation, every issue, every word which comes your way is divinely appointed. Take great care to glorify God.

> *But you are a chosen generation, a royal priesthood, a holy nation, His own special people, that you may proclaim the praises of Him who called you out of darkness into His marvellous light; who once were not a people but are now the people of God, who had not obtained mercy but now have obtained mercy.*
>
> *Beloved, I beg you as sojourners and pilgrims, abstain from fleshly lusts which war against the soul, having your conduct honourable among the Gentiles, that when they speak against you as evildoers, they may, by your good works which they observe, glorify God in the day of visitation.*
>
> *1 Peter 2:9-12*

Chapter 6: The Oil and Fine Linen

In the parable of the ten virgins, Jesus tells the story of the invitation to the wedding feast. The five wise virgins were admitted to the Wedding by the Bridegroom for the simplest of reasons: they took oil in their vessels and with their lamps. These wise virgins bought oil for themselves.

The foolish virgins ran out of oil and tried to borrow oil from the wise.

> *Then the kingdom of heaven shall be likened to ten virgins who took their lamps and went out to meet the bridegroom. Now five of them were wise, and five were foolish. Those who were foolish took their lamps and took no oil with them, but the wise took oil in their vessels with their lamps.*
>
> *But while the bridegroom was delayed, they all slumbered and slept.*
>
> *And, at midnight, a cry was heard: 'Behold, the bridegroom is coming; go out to meet him!' Then all those virgins arose and trimmed their lamps. And the foolish said to the wise, 'Give us some of your oil, for our lamps are going out.' But the wise answered, saying, 'No, lest there should not be enough for us and you; but go rather to those who sell, and buy for yourselves.'*
>
> *And while they went to buy, the Bridegroom came, and those who were ready went in with him to the wedding; and the door was shut.*
>
> *Afterward the other virgins came also, saying, Lord, Lord, open to us!' But he answered and said, 'Assuredly, I say to you, I do not know you.'*
>
> *Watch therefore, for you know neither the day nor the hour in which the Son of Man is coming.   Matthew 25:1-13*

How should this scripture be interpreted today?

The oil is a symbol of the Holy Spirit, but more than this, the oil reflects the anointing and the intimacy we develop in His Presence. How do we purchase the oil? What is the Lord trying to tell us about this oil and what does it mean? Spending time in His Presence is so important and yet so difficult. I cannot stress enough the importance of your life spent in His Presence.

The currency used for purchasing oil is the heart of worship. There is not only one last call for the last days, but there is one last call for Christians.

For those who seek Him daily and prioritise intimate meetings with the Lord, there is a change in the heart and spirit of that person:

Do you sit at the feet of Jesus in worship?

How much time do you spend with the Lord?

How focused and intense is your prayer time?

How intimate is your time with Him in His Presence?

Do you fast and pray?

Do you focus yourself on Him; are you sold out?

Are you desperate for Him?

Like all of you, I struggle with knowing and doing this one thing.

What is the One Thing?

Paul wrote to the Philippians about this One Thing, that he wanted to lay hold of Christ Jesus:

> *Not that I have already attained or am already perfected; but I press on, that I may lay hold of that for which Christ Jesus has also laid of me.*
>
> *Brethren, I do not count myself to have apprehended; but one thing I do, forgetting those things which are behind and reaching forward to those things which are ahead, I press toward the goal for the prize of the upward call of God in Christ Jesus.* *Philippians 3:12-14*

The Fine Linen

As you pursue your goals and make your journey, the Book of Revelation reveals the fine linen you are to wear in preparation for the marriage: that is, your righteous acts.

> *And I heard, as it were, the voice of a great multitude, as the sound of many waters and as the sound of mighty thunderings, saying, "Alleluia! For the Lord God Omnipotent reigns! Let us be glad and rejoice and give Him glory, for the marriage of the Lamb has come, and His wife has made herself ready."*
>
> *And to her it was granted to be arrayed in fine linen, clean and bright, for the fine linen is the righteous acts of the saints.*
> *Revelation 19:6-8*

Chapter 7: The Laodicean Church Age

Howard O. Pittman (1928 - 2019) served in the New Orleans Police Department for 26 years, prior to his first death in 1979. When Howard died at the age of 51 years, he was a police officer and a Christian, however God had appointed a time for Howard to die (Hebrews 9:27). Some of the following account is from Howard's books and some from other sources.[8]

On August 3, 1979, Howard Pittman suffered a physical death as the result of a massive internal haemorrhage due to an ulcer in his artery which had burst open - an aneurism.

In vivid detail, Howard describes his experience of standing before the Lord.

He appeared before the Lord in the Third Heaven where he pleaded for an extension of his physical life. There God showed him what kind of life of worship and service he had really led. Howard was a Laodicean-type Christian (see Revelation chapter 3). He was a good man and did many good works, but he had no idea that his good works were an abomination to the Lord.

When he died, Howard was taken by angels to see the battles in the spirit realm. While most of us cannot see this realm, God allowed Howard to see principalities, powers, demons, the hierarchy of the

---

[8] Howard O. Pittman's testimony was recorded by Mark Cowart on his YouTube channel here. https://www.youtube.com/watch?v=UKnwGMG7PHg

demons, angels, Heaven and Hell. Although he had died a horrible, painful death, he was permitted to return to his body with the instructions that he was to teach the church. He also saw this scripture written in Heaven before his eyes.

> *It is appointed for men to die once, but after this the judgment.*
> *Hebrews 9:27*

Howard was miraculously healed and sent back to this world with a message from Heaven.

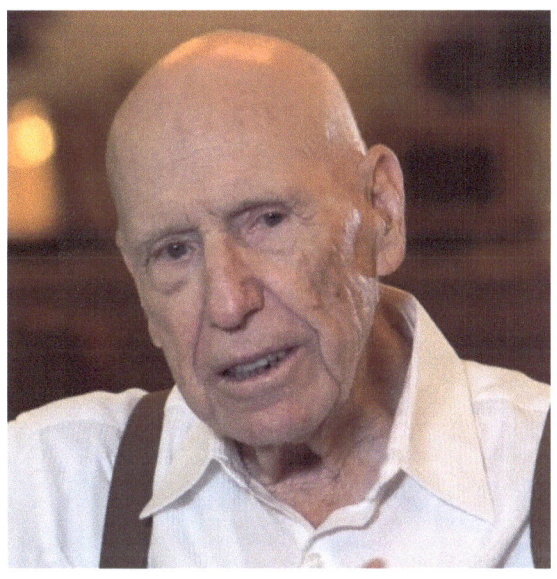

Following his first death experience, Howard left his job in law-enforcement and travelled all over the United States and to over 20 other countries (between 1980 and 2019).

He preached his testimony all over the world and wrote many books about his near-death experiences and the messages God gave him.[9]

---

[9] *Placebo* is a book written by Howard O. Pittman's about his life and can be read as a digital PDF book here https://www.howardpittman.org/product/placebo-digital-pdf-ebook/

You can search Howard's testimonies through videos available on YouTube. One such video was recorded towards the end of his life in 2015 and may be viewed here.[10] Howard was 87 years old at the time of these interviews and died four years later aged 91 years. He described the spiritual war on the church in John's vision:

> *It was granted to him (the Beast) to make war with the saints and to overcome them. And authority was given him over every tribe, tongue, and nation. All who dwell on the earth will worship him, whose names have not been written in the Book of Life of the Lamb slain from the foundation of the world. If anyone has an ear, let him hear.*   *Revelation 13:7-9*

This spiritual war will consist of an attack of the enemy (demons) upon the saints by their two predominant emotions: hate for all humans and fear of Satan (their supreme commander). While visiting the Lord, Howard was taught the following points to instruct the church:

We are now living in the Laodicean Church Age. The overwhelming majority of Christians are not genuine – in name only. The Laodicean Church Age is characterized by lukewarmness, materialism and a decline in spiritual fervour. This lukewarmness is reflected in a decline in spiritual zeal and a focus on worldly pursuits, rather than a genuine relationship with God. Unless the Christian church wakes up, God is going to spew them out of His mouth. He promised to do that, but He has given them a chance, if they wake up.

> *Not everyone who says to Me, 'Lord, Lord,' shall enter the kingdom of heaven, but he who does the will of My Father in heaven. Many will say to Me in that day, 'Lord, Lord, have we not prophesied in Your name, cast out demons in Your name, and done many wonders in Your name?'*
>
> *And then I will declare to them, 'I never knew you; depart from Me, you who practice lawlessness!'*
>
> *Matthew 7:21 - 23*

Your adversary is a personal and powerful adversary: Satan the Devil; he is Anointed. If you ever expect to have any of God's power manifest in your life, you're going to have to live the life, not just talk it. As it was in the days of Noah, so shall it be in the days of the coming of the Son of Man. Keep your eye on the Eastern Sky, because your Redemption draweth nigh. We have reached the days of Noah, once again. In history, and the Bible, we can see how it was in the days of Lord.

We see that mankind had but two priorities: wealth and pleasure. Everything else is secondary. That's the way it was in the days of Noah. He said it was going to be that day again.

Matthew was quoting John the Baptist when he said:

> *I indeed baptize you with water unto repentance, but He who is coming after me is mightier than I, whose sandals I am not worthy to carry.*
>
> *He will baptize you with the Holy Spirit and fire.*
>
> *His winnowing fan is in His hand and He will thoroughly clean out His threshing floor and gather His wheat into the barn; but He will burn up the chaff with unquenchable fire.*
>
> Matthew 3:11, 12

The baptism of the Holy Ghost is going to come with fire. He's going to burn up the chaff in the Christian. A lot of people think that the baptism of the Holy Spirit is evidenced by speaking in in tongues. The real evidence is the fire burning the chaff out of the individual and that's going to take tribulation. The fifth point is the baptism of the Holy Spirit, the true baptism of the Holy Spirit.

The fire is coming. The true baptism of the Holy Spirit is going to bring fire in the chaff for the life of the individual.

On 3rd August 1979, while Howard was judged to be dead and transported to hospital, there was a 15-minute span of time. During this time, he saw 2,000 people who had died, however only 50 saints out of 2,000 made it into Heaven (2.5%). Most of these people did not make it (97.5%). Howard saw 50 saints that went into heaven and that was the sum total of his Harvest on the planet Earth for 15 minutes span of time. Out of 2,000 people, 1,950 did not enter Heaven.

In Matthew, the Lord said, for many will say to me in that day, 'but Lord, Lord, have we not preached in your name? (Matthew 7:21-23).

Chapter 8: The Baptism of Fire

The *Baptism of Fire* is described by John the Baptist as a separate event in a person's life. And, here in Acts, we can see the same description:

> *And suddenly there came a sound from heaven, as of a rushing mighty wind, and it filled the whole house where they were sitting.*
>
> *Then there appeared to them divided tongues, as of fire, and one sat upon each of them. And they were all filled with the Holy Spirit and began to speak with other tongues, as the Spirit gave them utterance.*
>
> Acts 2:2-4

Now the early church experienced both the *Baptism of the Holy Spirit and Fire* as one experience. However, the fire element has been missing in the Pentecostal church. It has been missing for many years. *We should ask: why is this?*

Jesus said He came to send fire on the earth!

> *I came to send fire on the earth and how I wish it were already kindled!* Luke 12:49

How is fire obtained in our lives?

Jesus said that the Laodicean Church had to buy three things from Him. We have to buy gold refined in the fire if we want to be rich.

> *I counsel you to buy from Me gold refined in the fire, that you may be rich; and white garments, that you may be clothed, that the shame of your nakedness may not be revealed; and anoint your eyes with eye salve, that you may see. Revelation 3:18*

Towards the end of the 19th century and the beginning of the 20th century, it was common for those who were *Baptized in the Holy Spirit* to experience a *Baptism of Fire*, like the early church. Why has that experience, the *Baptism of Fire*, been lost?

Why do only a few experience this *Baptism of Fire*?

Let us review a few instances of the Holy Spirit moving in recent history.

The Latter Rain and Healing Revivals[10]

The Latter Rain and healing revivals constituted only two of many aspects of a widespread awakening occurring during the middle of this century. The healing revival was known for its emphasis upon healing, while the Latter Rain Movement was known for its use of the laying on of hands with prophecy. The healing revival precipitated the

---

[10] The Latter Rain and Healing Revivals **is described by Richard Riss**
https://lrm1948.blogspot.com/2013/05/the-latter-rain-movement-in-its-context.html

Latter Rain Movement, but both were really only two aspects of the same move of God.

The Post-war Awakening[11]

In late 1949, revival broke out on the Island of Lewis and Harris, the largest of the Outer Hebridean group in Scotland.[12] Indications of revival in the United States included the Forest Home College Briefing Conferences (1949) and the Pacific Palisades Conferences, at which scores of pastors and ministers of various denominations, only a few of whom were Pentecostal, gathered together several times a year for prayer and praise in an atmosphere of spiritual renewal.

Spontaneous revival was also breaking out on many college campuses. The revival at Wheaton College (February 5-12, 1950) received national publicity, appearing in the pages of *Time* and *Life* magazines.[13]

There were well over twenty other college revivals occurring at the same time.

The Healing Revival

However, before these events, the healing revival had already begun to surface.

Two of the earliest, and most influential, healing evangelists were William Branham and Oral Roberts. Other important figures included T. L. Osborn, Jack Coe, William Freeman, A. A. Allen, and

---

[11] https://lrm1948.blogspot.com/2013/05/the-latter-rain-movement-in-its-context.html
[12] https://www.youtube.com/watch?v=MXIZOSWvXaE
[13] https://revival-library.org/histories/1950-wheaton-college-revival/

David Nunn. Gordon Lindsay, who helped bring William Branham's ministry into widespread recognition, used his talent to supply the movement with a needed element of cohesiveness.

Branham's healing ministry began on 7 May 1946, when he had an angelic visitation in which he was told that he was to take the gift of divine healing to the people of the world.[14] Within five weeks he was conducting healing revivals in St. Louis and, before long, his meetings were attracting enormous crowds.

In 1947, Oral Roberts began his healing ministry. Branham testified that Roberts' "commanding power over demons, over disease and over sin was the most amazing thing he had ever seen in the work of God."

Young Brown, Jack Moore, William Branham, Oral Roberts and James Gordon Lindsay (1948)[15]

---

[14] https://william-branham.org/site/research/topics/angelic_visitation
[15] This photo was taken at a revival meeting in 1948, Kansas City. The photo is public domain and published in 1950. Copyright was not renewed. https://en.wikipedia.org/wiki/Healing_revival#Evangelists

Many of the revivalists of the Healing Movement became associated with <u>The Voice of Healing</u> magazine, published by Gordon Lindsay, the May 1952 issue of which had pictures on its cover of twenty healing evangelists. Two years previous to this time, as many as one thousand itinerant evangelists had attended a meeting sponsored by Gordon Lindsay in Kansas City.

Latter Rain Revival

The Latter Rain Movement was initiated, by William Branham's campaigns in Vancouver, British Columbia, Canada, in the fall of 1947. [16]

His demonstrations of the gift of healing accompanied by knowledge of the illnesses of those present made a deep impression on the teachers at Sharon Bible School in North Battleford, Saskatchewan, Canada. This precipitated revival at their school after their return from the Branham meetings.

The Sharon Orphanage and Schools sparked an explosion of revival among many Pentecostals. It spread quickly throughout North America and many places throughout the world, including the Middle East, India, Japan, Latin America, Africa, New Zealand, Australia, and Europe.

George Hawtin, 1948
President of Bethel Bible Institute in Saskatoon

---

[16] https://romans1015.com/latter-rain/

Beginning in November 1947, Hawtin led students through several months of Bible study, prayer, and fasting at *Sharon Children's Homes and Schools*.[17] Sharon consisted of three groups of students and faculty:

- A Bible school
- An orphanage
- A technical institute

By February 1948, the spiritual anticipation had reached such a peak at the Sharon School that they scheduled February 11-14, 1948, for there to be extended chapel services. On day two of the 4-day series of meetings, Thursday, February 12, Ernest Hawtin (George Hawtin's brother) wrote in the Sharon Star magazine what occurred.[18]

The 1948 revival (whatever one calls it: The Move of the Spirit, the Latter Rain Movement, etc.) began in February 1948 at the Sharon Orphanage and Schools in North Battleford, Saskatchewan, Canada.

> *Some students were under the power of God on the floor, others were kneeling in adoration and worship before the Lord. The anointing deepened until the awe was upon everyone.*
>
> *The Lord spoke to one of the brethren, 'Go and lay hands upon a certain student and pray for him.' While he was in doubt and contemplation one of the sisters who had been under the power of God went to the brother saying the same words, and naming the identical student he was to pray for.*

---

[17] https://romans1015.com/tag/sharon-schools-and-orphanage-revival/
[18] https://romans1015.com/tag/sharon-schools-and-orphanage-revival/

> *He went in obedience and a revelation was given concerning the student's life and future ministry.*
>
> *After this, a long prophecy was given with minute details concerning the great thing God was about to do. The pattern for the revival and many details concerning it were given.*
>
> *It seemed that all Heaven broke loose upon our souls, and Heaven came down to greet us.*
>
> *Soon, a visible manifestation of gifts was received when candidates were prayed over, and many, as a result, began to be healed, as gifts of healing were received.*
>
> *Day after day, the Glory and power of God came among us. Great repentance, humbling, fasting and prayer prevailed in everyone.*

The believers were praying for others with the laying on of hands and resulting in the expression of spiritual gifts by the person being prayed for. This led to people from all over the region coming to participate in the meetings, so that they too might receive these gifts that they had been praying so long to receive.

George Hawtin wrote about what he witnessed during this time:

> *During the past six weeks we have enjoyed a great visitation of the Spirit of God. Some of us have been praying for twenty years that the nine gifts of the Spirit would be restored to the Church. The Spirit of fasting and prayer has rested upon the whole school all winter.*
>
> *Finally, the great "Break Through" came and the spiritual gifts began to operate among us... The revival is spreading all over the province.*[19]

During that time period, a popular teaching swept through the charismatic / Pentecostal church, that the *Baptism of the Holy Spirit* can be received by Faith alone. The teaching asserted that no personal preparation was needed. You just had to have faith to receive the *Baptism of the Holy Spirit*. The *Baptism of the Holy Spirit* was thought to be the same as the *Baptism of Fire*.

While there was some truth in this teaching, it was not the whole truth. This period saw a revival and a renewed emphasis on the gifts of the Holy Spirit, including speaking in tongues and other Charismatic expressions.

Although many experienced the *Baptism of the Holy Spirit*, the element of fire, which signified purification and sanctification, was

---

[19] **Hawtins and Kirkpatrick w/Kopp (May 1949) Detroit mentioned** Sat, May 7, 1949 – 19 · *The Los Angeles Times (Los Angeles, California).* Newspapers.com

often missing. This lack of the *Baptism of Fire* led to issues of carnality and mixture within the movement.

The "1948 move of God" is remembered for its impact on the church, bringing about a restoration of spiritual gifts and a deeper understanding of the Holy Spirit's work in believers' lives. It also highlighted the need for a more profound experience of sanctification and purification through the Holy Spirit.

Sanctification

Many in the Holiness movement of the 19th century experienced a different move, which they called sanctification. It was a real experience. A life-changing experience that transformed them. They did not receive the baptism of the Holy Spirit and speak in tongues, but they experienced something which was very powerful and had a transforming effect upon their lives.

They called this experience *Sanctification.*

For people to experience Sanctification, much preparation was needed. They spent time searching their lives before God; they spent much time allowing the Holy Spirit to search their hearts. They would constantly place themselves on the altar of God, spiritually speaking, as an act of absolute surrender to the Lord. Through this process God really dealt with them; dealt with their heart and dealt with the problems of Purity in their lives. Primarily He was dealing with their absolute surrender to Him.

They had a saying, "when the last piece is laid upon the altar, the fire would fall." This was an allusion alluding to the altar that Elijah built on Mount Carmel.

When the last piece was placed upon the altar, the fire fell.

> *And it came to pass, at the time of the offering of the evening sacrifice, that Elijah the prophet came near and said, "Lord God of Abraham, Isaac, and Israel, let it be known this day that You are God in Israel and I am Your servant, and that I have done all these things at Your word. Hear me, O Lord, hear me, that this people may know that You are the Lord God, and that You have turned their hearts back to You again."*
>
> *Then the fire of the Lord fell and consumed the burnt sacrifice, and the wood and the stones and the dust, and it licked up the water that was in the trench. Now when all the people saw it, they fell on their faces; and they said, "The Lord, He is God! The Lord, He is God!"*
>
> *1 Kings 18:36-39*

Many in the Holiness movements experienced the *Baptism of Fire*. They called it an experience of sanctification, but it was very powerful and life changing.

This *Baptism of Fire* brought about an experience in their lives called Sanctification. This experience dealt with the nature of sin in their lives. The fire purged them during a great deep work within them and preparing the place for the Holy Spirit to dwell.

The Charismatic Move of God

In the late 60s in early 70s, another move of the Spirit came, which we called the Charismatic Move, and it was a great move of God in the Evangelical Churches and the Catholic Church. Many people received the Baptism of the Holy Spirit, across all denominations. However, there was one element missing and that was a fire. There was no *Baptism of Fire* and that resulted in much carnality and mixture.

During those years the word sanctification was very rarely heard.

The Seraphims are Coming with Fire

In a more recent vision, a prophetic man of God had a Vision with the Lord early one morning in 2007. The passage below is found in his book and some passages are replicated here.[20]

> *On July 1st, 2007, I got up early in the morning and sat down to pray when suddenly, without warning, I was in another realm, that of the spirit. I found myself watching the Lord picking up sticks and wood. He placed the wood in a small pile and then started another pile. The Lord then looked at me and asked, "Will you help me?" A little startled, I said yes, and began picking up wood, placing it into piles on the ground.*

---

[20] This testimony is found in the book *The First Principles: Foundations Necessary for Entering the Kingdom* © 2010 Neville Johnson Publisher Living Word Foundation

The Lord looked at each pile of wood and then blew on each pile. As He did this, each pile burst into flames.

The scene changed and I was high above America looking down with what seemed like a view you would get from an orbiting satellite. As I looked down, I saw fires starting all over the country. Many of these fires joined together and became much bigger.

One thing stood out; there was no smoke coming off the fires. I then began to see other nations where a similar thing was happening.

Again, I was down where the fires were burning and I turned to the Lord and asked, "What is happening?" At this level, I could plainly see many people in the fires praising God.

Then people began to emerge from the fire. They were glowing and their skin was smooth -- almost glass like – with not a wrinkle anywhere. I remember thinking beauty salons could make a fortune with this. The Lord looked at me and smiled, hearing what I was thinking. These people looked almost molten as they glowed with blue, white and red hues.

I asked, "Lord, what is this?" He answered, "You are seeing what I am about to do next. I will purify my people with fire!"

I then saw these people healing the sick. The Power of God was flowing through them unhindered as they were casting out demons and healing the people. I marveled at the authority they had. Their words instantly manifested what they spoke.

> *The Lord spoke saying, "Tell the people they must give themselves to Me: you will not be changed unless in humility and sincerity you come to Me and ask me to do it."*

Neville's experience in Heaven was to see these very awesome creatures, the Seraphim. They seemed fierce, yet benign. They stood by the throne of God and above it.

The Lord said, "These are My Seraphim" - they sounded like blow torches and were awesome, indescribable creatures. The Hebrew word Saraph means burning.

Just one in the midst of a church will start a revival. They will burn out the darkness of sin along with the results of sin in their lives.

I will baptize them with fire and then the world will see them burn with my love, justice and power."

Fire is not for cleansing of sin. Fire is for purging and refining; it deals with the consequences of sin in one's life, the pollution that sin has caused. It also deals with the demonic.

What is needed is the Blood, the Cross and the Fire:

- Blood for cleansing,
- Cross for dying to self and
- Fire for purging.

The Fire deals with soiled emotions, hurts, polluted minds, bad memories, spirit strongholds, body pollution and hereditary problems.

We're coming into that time period now. When the water baptism is taught in a way of absolute surrender to God, surrendering of Our Lives, surrender to God.

In Isaiah 4:4, when the Lord have washed away the filth of the daughters of Zion and purged the blood of Jerusalem from the midst by the spirit of judgment and by the spirit of burning, that word burning in the Hebrew is the word Seraph.

This preparation for the *Baptism of Fire* requires an absolute surrender of our lives; a seeking of God; the laying down of our lives. We need to ask him to bring the fire.

Those of you who've been already baptized in the Holy Spirit, now need to seek God for the *Baptism of Fire* to be added to that, so there will come an absolute purging and cleansing.

The *Baptism of Fire* will preserve a generation of Christians that will live through the greatest darkness the world has ever seen (see Isaiah 60:2).

> *And he shall sit as a refiner and purifier of silver: and he shall purify the sons of Levi, and purge them as gold and silver, that they may offer unto the LORD an offering in righteousness.*   *Malachi 3:3*

The fire burns out hurts, fears, inferiorities, hereditary problems, sexual abuse, mental health disorders and illnesses, inherited sins of the fathers and enemy strongholds in the minds of God's people.

The Outer Court, Inner Court and the Holy of Holies

The soul of today's Christians.

> *The Christian today is like an open garden with creepers climbing all over the entrance and weeds are growing around the way. The garden is overgrown and in a state of disrepair. This is the Church.*
>
> *Christ's shows great love for the church and yet He said, "This is the outer court of where most Christian's dwell."*

There is a room at the end of the garden. This room was covered and quite dimly lit. A candlestick on the left and a table opposite it with bread on it. This was the Holy Place of the tabernacle which Moses had built in the wilderness.

There is very little light in this place and a lot of smoke. The room was very smoky and the candlestick was giving off what seemed to be things that represented Holy and unholy things causing a pungent smell, a mixture of pure and impure.

The Holy Place

This was the area of the soul: mind, emotions and will. Bad thoughts, unclean thoughts, good thoughts, good feelings and bad.

Watchman Nee described the Christian soul in his book, *The Spiritual Man*.[21] He described the soul as the place you connect your intellect and emotions.

This book consists of three volumes of the great Chinese pastor-teacher Watchman Nee's classic work, based on Scripture and personal experience, on the spiritual life and spiritual warfare. This is a complete presentation on the workings of the human spirit and soul and body.

At the end of the room, there is an altar with a lot of smoke coming out of it along with a very small white vapor which had a nice smell. This was the Altar of Incense. There was very little incense represented by the white vapor, however, there was a lot of darker smoke.

There is much in the Church that is good, but God must do a much deeper work of cleansing.

The Lord threw some incense on the altar and a great white vapor ascended, lighting up the whole place. A veil parted behind the Altar of Incense.

The altar of incense, also known as the golden altar, was a crucial piece of furniture within the tabernacle and later the temple. It was located in the Holy Place, before the veil, and was used for burning incense daily. The rising smoke, along with the sweet fragrance of the incense, symbolized the prayers of the people ascending to God.

---

[21] *The Spiritual Man by Watchman Nee 1928. September 20, 1968 by Christian Fellowship Publishers.*

The altar of incense was situated in the Holy Place, directly in front of the curtain that separated it from the Holy of Holies.

Made out of acacia wood and overlaid with gold, the altar of incense stood the tallest of all the furniture in the Holy Place (a foot and a half square (46 cm) and three feet high (91 cm)). An ornamental gold rim like a crown circled the top with golden "horns" on each corner. The altar stood before the veil that separated the Holy of Holies from the Holy Place. The priest burned incense here, morning and evening, as he trimmed the lamps.

The Holy of Holies

As Christians move through the veil into the Holy of Holies, the Ark of the Covenant becomes central. Jesus dwells within our spirit in the secret place of the Most High.

The Ark of the Covenant was a sacred, golden-covered chest described as the Israelites' most holy object. It was designed to house the Ten Commandments and other sacred items, symbolizing the presence of God among the Israelites. According to the Bible, God commanded Moses to have it built at Sinai.

The Ark was made of acacia wood and overlaid with gold inside and out. It was 2.5 cubits long, 1.5 cubits wide, and 1.5 cubits high, which translates to approximately 132 cm long, 79 cm wide and 79 cm high.

It served as a container for the Ten Commandments and other holy items like Aaron's Rod and the Manna jar, though some believed it held only the Ten Commandments during King Solomon's time.

The Ark was a symbol of God's presence among the Israelites and was believed to have supernatural power.

> *It is time to dwell in the secret place of the Most High.*

What is about to occur in the Church, to those who are seeking all that God has for them, is the next move of God will include the fire of God that will transform people into a flaming fire.

Just as Jesus was transfigured, even so, the church will undergo a transfiguration experience where the light flowing from one's spirit will affect the whole being of man, transforming and renewing.

---

[22] This is a photo of the replica Ark of the Covenant at Brigham Young University, Utah. https://www.flickr.com/photos/88663091@N04/39116340194/

I have not met many people who have been *Baptised with the Fire of God.* Some have had deep intimacy with the Holy Spirit, but not many that would testify to the *Baptism of Fire.* One such man is Rodney Howard-Browne. The price for his testimony was great. The following is his personal testimony.

Hungry and Thirsty for God by Rodney Howard-Browne

I began to get hungry for God. In July of 1979, I cried out to God in sheer desperation. I wanted Him to manifest Himself to me and in me. I was hungry.

He told me that I had to hunger and thirst. At first said to Him, "Why don't You just give it to me? I have served You all my life. I have been a good boy. I haven't done this, I haven't done that, as others have. God, I deserve it."

He said, "I'm not a respecter of persons. You come the same way everyone else does. You come in faith and you get hungry and you desire it. Then I'll give it to you."

You have to desire it like a man who has been in the desert three days desires water. All he can cry for is water. If a man walks up to him and offers him half a million dollars, he will push him aside and shout, 'No, water, water, water!' He wants water more than life itself, because the only thing that is going to save him is water.

When you become desperate for the Holy Ghost in your life like that, so that you want nothing else, then He will come. There is something about a hungry and thirsty heart that will cause God's power to move over a million people and come to your house.

Baptism of Fire

As I prayed that day, I told the Lord, "Either You come down here and touch me, or I am going to come up there and touch You." I was desperate. I must have called out to God for about twenty minutes that day.

Suddenly the fire of God fell on me. It started on my head and went right down to my feet. His power burned in my body and stayed like that for three whole days. I thought I was going to die. I thought He was going to kill me.

I thought, He has heard my prayer, "Either You come down here and touch me or I will come up there and touch You," and now He has come down here and touched me and He is going to kill me and take me home.

I was really praying, "Lord, I am too young to die." In the fourth day, I am not praying, "O Lord, send your glory," I am praying, "Please lift it off me so that I can bear it."

I was plugged into heaven's electric light supply and, since then, my desire has been to go and plug other people in.

My whole body was on fire from the top of my head to the soles of my feet. Out of my belly began to flow a river of living water.

I began to laugh uncontrollably and then I began to weep and then speak with other tongues.

Drunk on the New Wine

I was so intoxicated on the wine of the Holy Ghost that I was literally beside myself. The fire of God was coursing through my whole being and it didn't quit. I began to realize why we would need a glorified body when we get to heaven. When the natural comes in contact with the supernatural, something has to give way and it's not going to be the supernatural.

He did finally lift that intense anointing off me, but it stayed lightly on me, that I was aware of, for two weeks. Because of that encounter with the Lord, my life was radically changed from that day on. [23]

How About You?

I was deeply moved by the desire of this man to receive more from Heaven.

---

[23] *This is an excerpt from Dr Rodney Howard Browne's testimony:*
https://www.drrodneyhoward-browne.com/rodney-howard-browne/the-testimony-of-dr-rodney-howard-browne/

Chapter 9: Is God Speaking to You?

How do you see the fire of God in your own life? Jesus said that He was sent to bring fire to us. For you may be at the beginning of this fire; you may be in the middle of this fire; you may think you are at the end of the fire.

> *"I came to send fire on the earth, and how I wish it were already kindled!*
>
> *"But I have a baptism to be baptized with, and how distressed I am till it is accomplished! Do you suppose that I came to give peace on earth? I tell you, not at all, but rather division.*
>
> *For from now on five in one house will be divided: three against two, and two against three. Father will be divided against son and son against father, mother against daughter and daughter against mother, mother-in-law against her daughter-in-law and daughter-in-law against her mother-in-law."*   Luke 12:49-53

However, there is a Baptism of Fire to come to each Christian, to each church and to the world. While we have seen in part, there is a greater Glory and a greater Fire to come.

My ongoing desire and prayer for you is that, as you read these stories and testimonies, you will form a hunger and longing for the Lord to be your one thing.

www.ingramcontent.com/pod-product-compliance
Lightning Source LLC
Chambersburg PA
CBHW042304150426
43197CB00001B/6